Abstracts

of

Gates County, North Carolina
Deeds

1828-1833

-Volume #5 -

Compiled by:
Mona Armstrong Taylor

Notes

This is my sixth volume in a series on the deeds of Gates
County, North Carolina and shows a great deal of movement by in-
habitants of the county to other counties and states during the
period of 1828-33. As in other volumes many deeds are on people
living in Nansemond County, Va. and Chowan and Hertford counties
in North Carolina, from which parts of Gates were taken when it
was formed in 1778.

I have given as much land description as seemed important
and include all names and places. All deeds end with "and back
to the first station," which I have left off in interest of time
and space.

I'm sure there are errors in names and initials as I and J
were often hard to distinguish between as were S and L. Daniel
and David were difficult to tell apart.

It is my hope that this book will be of help to those
having roots in Gates County.

                                              MJT

Page

5 11 Feb 1829--Simon Walters to Jesse Savage...$800...394 acres
which he lately purchased from Nathaniel Doughtie and which is
bounded by Barnes Goodman, Jesse Savage, Robert Wilson, Charles
Walters, Ann Jenkins, John Savage and heirs of David Parker...
                                                    Simon Walters
Jesse Wiggens
James Savage

6 11 Feb 1829--John V. Sumner, sheriff, to Jesse Savage...$36.13
lands of Nathaniel Doughtie, William Parker and Simon Walters to
comply with writ in which John H. Haslett (John Savage real plantiff) recovered for debts and lands of Nathaniel Doughtie, Abram
Parker and Daniel Parker...$429.95½ with interest from 30 Apr 1828
which Haslett recovered...
                                                Jno.V.Sumner
James Savage
Jesse Wiggens
Ben. Sumner

7 17 Feb 1829--Lemuel C. Moore of Pasquotank to Nathan Riddick...
$275...93 acres adjoining lands of Milton Eason running his line to
Catherine Creek Swamp up run to Joseph Hurdle's line to J. Brink-
ley's line...
                                                Lem.C.Moore
Aug. Moore

8 4 Jun 1828--Thomas Riddick to Kicheon Norfleet...$500...81 acres
on W side of Norfleet's Creek mill beginning at red oak near mouth
of White Pot Swamp...S down Honey Pot Swamp to Bennetts Creek to
Mills R. Fields line to Joseph Riddicks corner to run of White Pot
Swamp and S...
                                                Thomas Riddick
Wm.W.Riddick
Richard Cross

8 8 Dec 1828--Jethro, James A. and Thomas Ballard of Nansemond to
Whitmill Stallings...$400...160 acres on S side of Catherine Creek
adjoining lands of John Mitchell, Peter B. Minton and others, former-
ly known as Mills Roundtree tract...
                                                Jethro Ballard
Jno. Brinkley   Jas. A. Ballard
Benjamin Franklin   Thos.W. Ballard

9 22 Aug 1828--John and Benjamin Blanchard Sr. to Walton Freeman...
$30...10 acres beginning at pine a corner tree in Frederick Blan-
chard's line running old mill path to red oak and down path to pond..
                                                John Blanchard
A. Applewhite   B. Blanchard
Solloman R. Walton
Timothy Walton

10 2 Jan 1828--Joseph Gordon to Riddick Hunter...$475...150 acres
formerly belonging to Kedar Ballard and sold under deed of trust
by Tilly W. Carr, trustee, and another tract where dwelling house
stands on S side of Col. Hunter's Mill Pond adjoining lands of
Samuel Harrell's heirs, Joseph Harrells and others...

Jos. Gordon

James(x)Davis
Jordon Parker

10 28 Jan 1829--Noah Felton to David Riddick...$200...33 acres known
by name Thomas Old Field beginning at white oak on outer edge of Gum
Branch a corner tree in Riddick's line to a sweet gum a corner tree
between Samuel Felton and said Riddick...

Noah Felton

W. Riddick
Thos.B.Hunter

11 21 Nov 1828--George Kittrell to Jonathan Williams, Levi Rogers,
Daniel Williams, Henry G. Williams, James Parker, Hardy Cross, William Cross and Levi Creecy, trustees...6/7 acre beginning at fork of
road on Willeys, Williams and Kittrells corner, down road to hickory
and black gum--S to a post oak a corner tree W to Willey's line...
to build Kittrell's Meeting House as a house of worship for members
of Methodist Church of USA...

George Kittrell

Willis F. Riddick
Blake Baker

11 13 Nov 1812--William Luffman of Princess Anne County to Ezekiel
Trotman of Camden...200 pds...5 acres on Sandy Cross binding on lands
of Joseph and Isiah Riddick and Dr. Baker and 29 acres binding on
lands of Edward Only, Barnaba Nixon and main road...

William Luffman

Phillip Luffman
Sophia Scott Dauge

13 16 Feb 1829--Frederick Blanchard to Benjamin Blanchard...$1.00
50 acres of land on which he lives joining lands of William Blanchard and others, 2 feather beds and furniture, household and kitchen furniture, 1 horse, 1 cow, 1 yearling...and to pay $159 which
said Frederick is indebted to Henry Bond...

Fred. Blanchard

M. Roberts

B. Blanchard
Henry Bond

14 17 Nov 1828--George Freeman to Timothy Walton...$1.00 and to
secure notes of John Mitchell and said Freeman to John Roberts
for $72 and $35 and one to Miles Welch of Chowan for $30...1 mare
and colt, 1 young horse, 1 gig, yoke of oxen, 8 head cattle, 11
head sheep, 30 head hogs, 1 ox cart of wheat and 1 horse cart of
wheat...

George Freeman

Frederick Jones
John H. Edwards

16 16 Jan 1829--James Phelps to James Costen...two tracts of land

for becoming security for notes: $230 to Walton Freeman, two $50
to James Lassiter and $40 to John Felton. First tract of 25 acres
whereon said Phelps lives joins lands of Frederick Jones and Elisha
Hunter and other tract of 100 acres he bought of James Howard, it
being the dower or 1/3 of his wife, Gilly, formerly belonging to
Henry Walton Sr., dec...and 1 Negro woman Cloe...

                                    James Phelps
Jos. Gordon   James Costen

17 7 Jan 1824--James Piland to Seth Piland...$300...76½ acres on
which Seth now lives bounded by lands of James Goodin and Prior
Savage, Mills Piland, A. Harrell and William Piland...

                                  James Piland
Reubin Piland
Isaac Piland

17 10 Jan 1829--Seth P. Morgan & Samuel R. Morgan to Abraham Morgan...$1200...140 acres beginning at pine corner of said Morgans and
Seth Benton running line of marked trees to main run of Bennetts Creek
and down creek to mouth of Middle Swamp up swamp to main road...

                              Seth P.(x)Morgan
John W. Parker   Samuel R.(x)Morgan
Seth R. Morgan
William Parker

18 1 Feb 1829--Benjamin Newsome of Southampton to Frederick Lassiter
$100...50 acres beginning at cypress in Coleman Branch at the mouth
in Watery Swamp up branch SE to pine to corner of Demsey Blanchards
old line to Watery Swamp...

                              Benjamin Newsom
Ben. L. Newsome
Alexander(x)Marshall

19 4 Mar 1828--Ann N. Harvey to John D. Pipkin...$133.33 1/3 ...
40 acres beginning at sweet gum on edge of Goffs Swamp SW to large
popular on swamp to a dead pine SE to a cedar to W side of swamp
to a new corner between said Harvey and said Pipkin to a post on
road leading from road to courthouse...

                              Ann N. Harvey
I.R. Riddick
Ben. Wynns

20 12 Jan 1829--Samuel R. Morgan and Abraham Morgan to John Pruden
$1.00 and to secure debt of $200...50 acres beginning at white oak
corner tree bounded by said Abraham's line W to pine, corner tree
between Abraham and Seth Benton to main road and along road to Middle
Swamp to large gum and across field and N...

Seth R. Morgan   Samuel P.(x)Morgan
William Parker   Abraham Morgan
John W. Parker   John Pruden Sr.

21 14 Feb 1829--Kedar Taylor to Humphrey Parker...$62.50...25 acres

beginning at a small persimmon stump in branch, said Parker's corner
in John Barnes line SW to an elm NW and then NE to Taylors corner
to Barnes line...

Kedar Taylor

Dempsey Knight
Benjamin Knight
John Mathews

22 24 Nov 1828--Miles Benton to Robert Wilson...$50...tract of land
that he inherited from his father, Jethro Benton, beginning at a
pine a corner of No.2 and No. 4 in division...NW to a black gum to
a sweet gum in Cow Swamp down swamp to small cypress in Mare Branch
and SE...

Miles(x)Benton

Nathaniel Doughtie
Harrison(x)Doughtie
Blake Baker

22 19 Nov 1828--Robert Wilson to Miles Benton...$50...20 acres in
Mare Branch beginning at pine in Big Mare Branch SW to red oak,SE
to small old field and around edge...

Robert Wilson

Nathaniel Doughtie
Blake Baker

23 5 Aug 1828--Nathaniel Doughtie to Robert Wilson...$150...41
acres beginning at black gum in Isaac Walters and Hardy D. Parker's
corner on Parkers line NE to dead pine stump to Parker's Mill Swamp
and S to Mare Branch and up swamp...

Nathaniel Doughtie

Isaac H. Jenkins
Miles(x)Benton

23 15 Dec 1828--James Piland to son, Mills for love and affection
all improvements on plantation betwixt a plantation of said Mills
and John Worrell's to be moved off at any time...

James Piland

24 29 Dec 1828--Henry G. Williams to Miles Parker...$30...25 acres
beginning at water oak in Levin Cuff's line until it intersects
with Kicheon Norfleets along his line to said Miles line to Williams
line...

H.G.Williams

James Parker
Hardy Cross

24 22 Nov 1828--Richard H. Cross of Montgomery County, Ala. to
Hardy Cross of Gates...$90...45 acres the tract of land my father,
John Cross, dec. owned adjoining lands of Hillory Willey, John
Willey and others...

Richard H. Cross

H.G. Williams
William Cross

25 1 Jan 1829--John Pruden Jr. to John Mathews...$325...53 acres

beginning at small white oak in David Riddick's line corner of
John Pruden Sr. SE to tall pine--Moses Newsom's corner to Seth
Benton's line to beach...

John Pruden Jr.

William Hudgins
Isiah Mathews

26 27 Jan 1829--George Costen to John Matthews...$450...37½ acres
beginning at stump near end of lane near John Matthews house to
corner tree between William and John P. Hudgins and N to corner
tree down lane to John P. Hudgins N to main road...

George Costen

Ro. Riddick
Riddick Mathews

27 5 Jun 1828--Thomas Riddick to son, John...two small Negro boys,
Sam and Toney...

Thos. Riddick

Jno. Riddick
Wm.L.Boothe

27 8 Jul 1828--Thomas Hare of Nansemond to James Morgan...$50...
84 acres bounded on E by land owned by said Morgan N by main road
leading past Morgans house on W and S by land owned by Charles Jones,
Jacob P. Jones and others and part allotted to him in division of
his fathers estate...

Thomas Hare

John C. Jenkins
Jethro A. Jenkins

28 7 Jan 1829--William Cowper of Virginia to John Hoffler...$500
128 acres N side of Baylis Swamp formerly belonging to Col. Jesse
Eason, dec. and which he heired from his father, John Cowper, dec.
beginning at white oak on N side of run of swamp on Vineyard Point
down run and E to edge of main desert so as to include Vineyard
Point and then N to John Small's line and W to Ellis corner and
S to edge of Baylis Swamp at high water and to edge of Mill Dam...

William Cowper

R.H. Ballard
James T. Freeman

29 13 Feb 1829--William Sears and wife, Permelia, to Exum Jenkins
$125...172 acre lot which was set apart to Joseph Speight begin-
ning in road in Robert Saunders line SW to a maple to dead pine in
Hooks Pond SW to a corner pine on W side of old road on edge of Mill
Pond...

William Sears

W.W. Cowper
Kicheon Norfleet

29 1 May 1823--William W. Riddick, sheriff, to William Arnold...
$1.00...25 acres belonging to Josiah Riddick bounded by land of
John Brothers heirs, Va. line and Abram Riddick--sold by court

writ brought by Edward Arnold to recover $40 debt...

Wm.W.Riddick

29 17 Jan 1829--John Hofler to James T. Freeman...$1.00 and to
make safe $200 debt for which John Hinton and Garrett Hofler are
bound to William Cowper of Va. and another for $200 for land he
bought of William Cowper...on Vinyard Point running to edge of
desert to John Small's line to Baylis Swamp and Mill Dam...

John Hofler

Reuben Hinton
Henry D. Lassiter

31 1 Dec 1828--David Harrell of Perquimans to John Alpin...$400
125 acres whereon his father, Theopolis Harrell, now lives adjoining lands of said Alpin, Abraham Harrell and others...

David Harrell

Jos. Gordon

32 13 Dec 1828--Jesse Pearce to Solloman Eason...$175...56 3/4
acres being part of tract formerly belonging to his father, William
Pearce, and to his brother, William Jr., of which said Jesse bought
joining lands of Nathan Ward, heirs of Isaac Riddick, dec., Josiah
Riddick and others...

Jesse(x)Pearce

J. Riddick
Abner Eason

33 4 Feb 1828--Noah Hinton and wife, Elizabeth, to James Boothe...
$80...17½ acres adjoining lands of each side of said Boothe and ly-
ing on main road--it being land drawn by Elizabeth in division of
her father's estate...

Noah Hinton
Elizabeth(x)Hinton

Jno.Walton
David Parker
   Henry Gilliam and John Walton, justices, testified Elizabeth
signed deed freely.

34 17 Feb 1829--Moses L. Newsome and wife, Martha, of Hertford to
John Mathews...$220...52½ acres beginning at corner pine in David
Riddick's line to said Mathews line to Seth Benton's line...

Moses Newsome

Wm.L.Boothe
Martha E. Newsome

Pryor Savage

34 19 Oct 1818--Demsey Eure of Edgecomb to Mills Eure...$350...
Negro boy, Jim...

D. Eure

35 25 Apr 1829--William, Thomas and John B. Walton; Nathan Nixon
and wife, Sarah; Elizabeth, Timothy, Mildred, Mary Ann and Joseph
Walton to Andrew Baker...$1.00...150 acres where on George Freeman
lived...and to comply with indenture made between said Freeman and
Timothy Walton 27 Jan 1823 and to make safe to John T. Benton $191.16
for which he was bound to Charles Johnson of Chowan by note signed
by George Freeman, John T. Benton and John Hofler and another note

dated 1 Dec 1822 for $441.15 for which John T. Benton and Frederick
Jones were bound to Timothy Freeman...   W. Walton
                                                       Thos. Walton
                                                       John B. Walton
Milton Eason   Nathan Nixon
William (x)Simpson   Sarah Nixon
                                                       Elizabeth Walton

37 20 Feb 1819--Elisha Harrell to Mills Eure...$412.50...Negro girl,
Aga, 13 years old...
                                                       Elisha Harrell
Jesse Taylor
Stephen Eure

37 4 Jan 1815--Daniel Southall to Henry Gilliam...$500...100 acres
on N side of road leading from courthouse to Coles Creek Branch beginning on roadside at dec. Gilliam's line and binding on his line
to Willis Brown's line and along his line to George Williams line and
back to road...   Daniel Southall
Wm.C.Brooks
John W. Southall

38 May Ct. 1824--Henry Riddick to Henry Gilliam...$80...1 acre on
main road from Suffolk to Edenton, purchased from estate of James
Meltier, dec.   Henry Riddick
I.W. Riddick
Rt. Parker

38 28 Feb 1825--John O. Hunter to Henry Gilliam...$300...100 acres
adjoining lands sold by late Isaac Hunter, dec. to William Saunders
and now property of Micajah Reed and lands formerly belonging to
Enoch Williams, dec. and lands of Elisha Harrell, dec...
                                                       John O. Hunter
T. Saunders
Martha Gilliam

38 15 Apr 1828--Sally Brown to Henry Gilliam...$55...11 acres ad-
joining said Gilliam's land and James Brown and a piece said Gilliam
purchased from James Brown...
                                                       Sally (x) Brown
Will C. Brooks
Martha Gilliam

38 31 Dec 1829--Whitmill Stallings and Andrew Baker transfer to
Walton Freeman all claim of debts against estate of Timothy Freeman,
dec. now defending in court...
Open Court   .

39 13 Aug 1822--Willis Brown to son, James...50 acres being a
tract purchased of James Brown and part of a tract purchased of
George Piland, beginning at red oak a corner tree of John Brown
and said James and running along H. Gilliams line to Sally Brown...
                                                       Willis(WB)Brown
H. Gilliam
Pryor Savage

40 10 Jan 1829--John Gatling to Abraham Parker...$600...3 acres
land whereon he lives and purchased of John D. Pipkin, adjoining
lands of Jesse Brown, Henry Gilliam and John D. Pipkin...

Jno. Gatling

H. Gilliam
W.G. Daughtery

40 20 Nov 1828--John D. Pipkin to John Gatling...$115...3 acres
land beginning at main road at Jesse Brown's corner running on
his line to H. Gilliam's and on Gilliam's line to a popular N and
down Pipkin's line to an oak stump on main road...

Jno. D. Pipkin

H. Gilliam
W.G. Daughtry

41 26 May 1918--Richard Morris of Louisa Co., Va. to Willie Mc-
Pherson of Camden...$400...1580 acres in Great Dismal Swamp, a part
of what is known as John Fontain's 6000 acre patent, derived by
said Morris by purchase from William and John Fontaine...

Richard Morris

Thomas Poindexter and Pleasant Hackell, justices for Louisa County,
Virginia, certified the deed and Richmond Terrell and Horatio G.
Winston attested to its execution...

42 1 Aug 1828--William Sears to William Wills Cowper...$450...150
acres beginning at post oak on E side of road to Winton to edge
of swamp to white oak and down run of swamp to Hackley Swamp branch..
John Brady   William Sears

43 14 Jul 1827--John G. Wilson and wife, Mary, of Hertford to William
Harrell of Gates...$25...10 acres, it being their part of lands of
Henry Harrell, dec. and is Lot No. 2 in division...
Noah Harrell   John G. Wilson
Edward G. Riddick   Mary Wilson

43 15 Oct 1827--Abraham Harrell and Henry Pugh attested Mary Wilson
signed deed freely...

44 26 Dec 1827--Noah Hinton and wife, Elizabeth, to Sally Lewis...
$35...½ of land sold by Seth Nowell and wife to Sally and Eliza-
beth Lewis, formerly being place where William Hinton Sr. lived
and died and is part drawn by Polly Nowell in division of land betwixt the Lewis heirs and said Sally Lewis...
H. Gilliam   Noah Hinton
J. Walton   Elizabeth(x)Hinton
    Henry Gilliam and John Walton attested Elizabeth Hinton signed
deed freely...

45 18 Dec 1827--John Sparkman and wife, Nancy, to David Umphlett...
$67...30 acres beginning at red oak a corner of Riddick Gatling's
and Dempsey Eure's running Gatling's line N to black gum thence on
said line to a corner W binding on Susan Beeman's to a white oak to
Dempsey Eure's corner and E...

John Sparkman
Nancy(x)Sparkman

Benjamin Beeman
Charney(x)Umphlett

45 7 Feb 1822--Stephen Rowe and wife, Margaret, to Peter Piland...
100 pds...165 acres bounded by William Cowper, Isaac Pipkin, William M. Harvey and Peter Piland, which was conveyed by Richard and
Elvey Odom and George W. Hill and wife to Edward Piland; which was
devised to Margaret Piland, now Margaret Rowe by will of Edward Piland, dec...

Stephen Rowe
Margaret Rowe

Elisha Piland
Susanna Piland

46 20 Aug 1824--Thomas Hare to Elisha Thomas Hare...$145...73
acres on S side of Josiah Riddick's Mill Pond beginning in Thomas
Parkers line NE along Parker's line to Thicket Swamp...down swamp
to gum trees and binding on James Morgan's land...

Thomas Hare

Mills R. Field
John W. Odam

47 20 Sep 1827--John V. Sumner, sheriff, to Abraham Morgan...$600
190 acres belonging to Seth Morgan and bounded by lands of Abraham
Morgan, Seth Benton, Micajah Riddick heirs and land of Mrs. Jane
Gregory lying on Bennetts Creek and Middle Swamp. Sold by several
court writs brought by Abraham Morgan...

John V. Sumner

I.R. Riddick

47 13 Aug 1822--Willis Brown to son, William, 56 acres purchased
of Jesse Parker 15 June 1799...

Willis(WB)Brown

H. Gilliam
Pryer Savage

48 13 Aug 1822--Willis Brown to daughter, Sally, 42½ acres purchased
from Willis, Mary, Nancy, Eliza and James Brown and James Parker, adjoining lands of Henry Gilliam, James Brown and William Piland...

Willis(WB)Brown

H. Gilliam
Pryer Savage

48 22 Nov 1828--Thomas Riddick to son, John, 350 acres of woodland
whereon said Thomas now lives...

Thomas Riddick

Riddick Cross
Mary Ann Kittrell

49 1 May 1829--Walton Freeman to Mary Hudgins...$395.51...91 acres
purchased at sheriff's sale and belonged to Frederick Blanchard beginning at stake on road leading from courthouse to Minton's Store
and along road to chinquapin tree to bridge on road across Mill Pond
S to Mirey Branch to land belonging to Henry Bond...

Walton Freeman

A. Darden
Tim. Walton

50 15 Jan 1829--Benbury Walton to John B. Walton...$422.12...Negroes
Lucy, Penny and Rachael and child, Cherry, which he purchased of
John P. Hudgins August last...

Benbury Walton

Jos. Riddick
Richard Hays

50 15 Jan 1827--John Jones and wife, Nancy, to John B. Walton...
$120...40 acres on main road leading from courthouse to Sunsbury
beginning at main road in run of branch near residence of Robert
Parker on S side of road running up branch and binding on lands of
said Parker and back to road--formerly belonging to Amos Lassiter,
dec....

Jos. Riddick
Richard Hays

                                              John Jones
                                              Nancy Jones

51 25 Apr 1829--John V. Sumner, sheriff, to Joseph Riddick...$701.10
for two tracts of land belonging to Isaac S. Riddick, dec. bounded by
lands of Abraham Hurdle, Joseph Riddick, Soloman Eason and others.
Sold by court writ brought by John Roberts and Jethro H. Riddick
against estate of Isaac S. Riddick for debts...

                                              Jn. V. Sumner
James W. Riddick

52 21 Oct 1826--James Gordon to a coloured man, Sipes, for good will
and meritorious acts...use of field whereon he now lives for his natural life. Sipes is late property of Isaac Costen...

George Costen
David Costen
                                              James Gordon

52 12 Jun 1828--John Roberts to Elisha Robertson...$150...30 acres
on which Jethro Reed now lives, bounded on N by Bagley's land on S
by Mrs. Lavina Parker's land, on W by said Robertson's land and on
E by road leading to Parker's Landing which separates it from Clement
Hill's land...

                                              John Roberts
M. Roberts
Henry B. Lassiter

53 17 Nov 1828--Harrison Doughtie to John V. Sumner...$1.00 to
indemnify Richard H. Ballard and Riddick Matthews security bond
to Joseph Riddick for $346.50...Negroes Peter, Jim and Lydia,
yoke of oxen, ox cart and wheels, horse cart and wheels, bay mare,
7 head of cattle, 3 feather beds, bedsteads and furniture, desk,
walnut beaufot, walnut table and 2 pine chairs...

                                              Harrison(x)Doughtie
Nath'l Doughtie

54 5 Jan 1829--Andrew Baker to Josiah Overman of Pasquotank...$450
60 acres land adjoining Abram Spivey's line on E, Nathan Cullens on
S, Timothy Walton on W and David Hobbs line on N...

                                              Andrew Baker
Thos. L. Spivey
David(x)Hobbs

54 27 May 1828--Benjamin Barnes of Jasper County, Ga. having moved
appoints Etheldred Cross as his attorney to dispose of land belong-
to him having fallen into his possession by death of sister, Milly
Bond, she having died without issue...

                                              Benj. Barnes
Jesse Loyall, justice of peace, was a witness and Alex. R. Buchannon,
clerk, of Jasper Court attested to signature and it was certified by
Bennet Crawford.

55 12 Nov 1828--Etheldred Cross, by power of attorney for Benjamin
Barnes of Jasper Co., Ga., to Richard Odom...$88...44 acres that
belonged to Milly Bond, formerly Milly Barnes, whose heirs appear
to be Benjamin Barnes, Charity Cross and heirs of Ethel'd B. Gatling
--Lot No. 2 and part of division of land into three parts...on
Capt. Richard Odom's line to large pine a corner of said Odom and
Jacob Odom NE to sweet gum...
                                              Ethel'd Cross
Jacob Odom
Elisha Williams

56 18 Nov 1829--Mills and James R. Riddick and Jethro Sumner, John
V. Sumner and James Gatling to John Roberts...$1.00 ...200 acres
and lot where courthouse sits and Negroes Old Frank, Mourning and
children, John, Maria, Sarah and Marcipa and Louisa and child, Davy..
to secure note of $2769.68 to John Roberts. Land belongs to Mills
Riddick where he resides and adjoins lands of Henry Gilliam, Reuben
Harrell, John Beeman and others...
                                              Mills Riddick
J. Walton   J.R. Riddick
B. Sumner

57 20 May 1829--Jason Holland to James Gardner, both of Nansemond,
$180...94 acre Wainoke Ferry Tract...that portion of land that was
allotted to Mildred Howell, dec. and conveyed by Joseph Holland, who
intermarried with said Mildred, to Jason Holland by deed...beginning
at post oak on river bank a corner of Matilda Rawls thence along a
line of marked trees to a bay in a small branch a corner of Edward
Howell's lot up branch binding on Edward and Demsey Howell's lot
and by line of marked trees to black oak in state line and binding
on Wiley Parker's line and state line due W to holly on Blackwater
River bank and binding on river...includes ferry, ferry flat and
fishery...
                                              Jason Holland
W.M. Jones

57 30 Jul 1828--Mary Lewis to John Lewis...$100...Negro boy, Frank,
7 years old...
                                              Mary(x)Lewis
William Gatling

58 22 Nov 1827--Jacob Eason Sr. to son, Jacob J. 100 acres beginning at a pine in John Felton's line a corner tree N to Cabbin Swamp
to a gum E to Elisha Riddick's to Moses Hurdles to John Feltons W...
                                              Jacob(E)Eason
John Polson
Moses (H)Hurdle
59 2 May 1829--Jane Bacus to Simmonds Roundtree...$13...12 acres
adjoining John Mathews, Benjamin Hays and others...it being all my
interest in land of Robert Parker, dec....
                                              Jane(x)Bacus
H. Gilliam
W. Hudgins

59 9 Oct 1828--John Eure to Joseph Smith...$40...6 acres on Cypress
Swamp beginning at poppaw gum near run to a dogwood near side of

marsh across neck of land to post oak down run of Little Cypress
and down main run...
                                                      John(x)Eure

Benj'm Beeman
Daniel Pierce

60 17 Mar 1829--Benjamin Knight to Demsy Knight...$16...8 acres
beginning at red oak nigh main road that leads to Suffolk running
SE to chinquapin oak a corner tree in old line formerly dividing
lands of James Knight, dec.and William Arnold and now said Demsy's
line SW running old line to white oak a corner of said Demseys and
John Benton...to an old oak blowed up...NW to road...
                                                      Benjamin Knight

Ethe'd Matthews
John Sparkman

61 3 Apr 1829--Miles Parker to Jonathan Williams...$110...41 acres
on N of lands of Henry G. Williams and E by Levin Cuff, S by Kicheon
Norfleet and W by lands of Jonathan Parker...
                                                      Miles Parker
James Figg
Anson Williams

62 29 Sep 1827--Elisha Eure to Jethro Eure...$120...my crop of corn
on plantation where I now live, 12 head hogs and 2 feather beds...
Simm's Roundtree   Elisha Eure

62 25 Mar 1829--Demsey Vann to Jesse Matthews...$250...60 acres
whereon he now lives adjoining lands of Josiah Riddick of Virginia
and others and formerly belonging to William Brinkley...
Jos. Gordon   Demsey Vann
M. Norfleet
John Alpin

63 27 Mar 1829--Joseph Gordon, trustee for Demsey Vann, $1.00 to
secure to him payment as trustee for tract of land 4 Nov 1824 described in above deed...

63 24 May 1828--Mills Riddick, clerk, to Seth and Augustus Morgan
$851...200 acres, the Duke Tract, adjoining Abraham Duke and others
on petition of heirs of Richard B. Gregory...
                                                      Mills Riddick
John Willey
Timothy Walton

64 10 Feb 1829--William Sears to Demsey Parker...$183.75...145
acres beginning at Thomson Bridge on Mrs. Harvey's Mill Swamp up
swamp to Jonathan Parker's line corner water oak thence along a
line of marked trees to Mrs. Harvey's line W to corner pine and NE
to road leading from courthouse to Virginia...
                                                      William Sears
John Willey
Harrison Vann

64 3 Dec 1828--Timothy Walton to Abraham Spivey...$175...25 acres
beginning at Suffolk Road called Muddy Cross running with David
Hobbs line to Andrew Baker's line then with his line to road leading from crossroads to courthouse--across road to a red oak a corner of said Baker's land to Nathan Cullens to small white oak to
Suffolk road...

                                                    Timothy Walton

Thomas Harrell
Andrew Baker

65 10 Oct 1828--Easther Mitchell to John Mitchell...$100...Negro
woman, Lett, which fell to me by will of husband, Richard...

                                                 Easter Mitchell

B.F. Hallsey

65 12 Mar 1829--David Cross to Willis Cross...$100...33½ acres
beginning at pine in Flat Branch that runs into Pine Swamp, William Hooks corner running his patent line down branch to mouth of
Old Orchard Branch and up center...

                                                 David Cross

Nath'l Eure
Martha Eure

66 22 Nov 1828--Wiley Cross of Nansemond to Robert Rogers...$170
...71 acres beginning at William Lee's line at small spruce pine
corner on Edward Howell's thence a N course a line of marked trees
on said Howell's line to run of Beech Swamp up run of swamp to
James Barnes line along Barnes line S to William Lee's thence on
said Lees line and W...

                                       Wiley Cross

William Lee
Francis Duke

66 13 Nov 1828--Henry Willey and wife, Peninah, to James Williams
$35...25 acres that Henry Copeland purchased at sheriff's sale and
is land that belonged to William Warren, which was sold under a
virtue of an execution by Jethro Sumner's, sheriff. Said Henry
and Peninah Willey drawed it in division of land that belonged to
Henry Copeland, dec. and adjoins lands of Thomas Barnes, dec.,
Richard Barnes, Richard Odom, James Williams and others...

                                       Henry Willey

Jethro Willey
Susan L. Copeland   Peninah Willey

   George Kittrell and William Goodman testified that Peninah
signed deed freely.

68 10 Feb 1829--Etheldred Cross and wife, Charity, to Richard Odom
$88...44 acres beginning at corner pine standing in Richard's line
near Vann place running Odom's line to pine near old schoolhouse to
sweet gum thence binding on land of heirs of Ethel'd B. Gatling...

                                    Etheldred(x)Cross

Willis Cross   Charity Cross
Jacob Odom
Abm. Cross

14

69 10 Feb 1829--John Kelly and wife, Milly, to Walton Freeman...
$24...6 acres beginning at sassafras near Frederick Blanchard's
line and along his line to Miry Branch to Mill Pond...
                                                    John Kelly
Robt. Stallings   Milly(x)Kelly
Henry Stallings
    Joseph Riddick and Peter B. Minton, justices, testified that
Milly signed freely.

70 19 May 1829--Henry Riddick and wife, Lydia A., to John Brady...
$160...95 acres beginning at a pawpaw tree a corner of Kindred Par-
ker's standing in Peterson's Swamp, thence along said Parker's line
to his corner to William Sears line, a water oak, along Sears line
a line of marked trees to Parkers and John Brady's corner and run of
swamp...
                                                    Henry Riddick
David Parker   Lydia A. Riddick
Kindred Parker
    Henry Gilliam and John Walton testified that Lydia signed freely.

71 5 Feb 1828--Jethro Sumner and wife, Nancy, of Nansemond to George
W. Lawrence...$1500...76 acres beginning in Cypress Swamp at mouth
of small branch a corner of William Davidson's thence up said branch
to sweet gum SE to red oak and NE to a pine Elijah Hare's corner and
SE to corner of Lewis Eure's and Speights to Spring Branch in Joshua
Lang's line and down branch...
Open Court   Jethro Sumner

72 19 Aug 1828--William Hudgins to George Costen...$1480...110½
acres...two parcels of land beginning at fork of road near John
Mathews house running road N to Micajah Riddick's line and along
his line to white oak at 6-ft. ditch to main roan and John P. Hudgins
James Lassiter
Jet.H. Riddick   W. Hudgins

73 28 Feb 1829--William D. Rascoe of Chowan, attorney of Burton
Hathaway of Tyrell to Ester Mitchell, all of said Hathaway's interest in Negro man, Tom, 30 years old, which descended to him by
will of Richard Mitchell...$25...
                                                    Burton Hathaway
Simon Stallings   by Wm. D. Rascoe

73 12 Feb 1827--Mills Eure to Lewis Eure...$400...Negro woman, Han-
nah, and her boy, Giles...
                                                    Mills Eure
Samuel Eure

74 12 Nov 1829--Jesse Hudgins, of the first part, James R. Riddick
of second part , security for Henry Gilliam of the third part...$1.00
to Henry Gilliam; Negroes, Alexander, Tamer, Jane Drew, Charles and
Mary; sorrell stead horse...to hold property in trust for a note to
Jethro Willey for $360 and one to John Roberts for $664...
                                                    Jesse Hudgins
                                                    I.R. Riddick
Jeptha Fowlkes   H. Gilliam

75 4 Feb 1822--Kedar Ballard, sheriff, to Humphrey Parker...$180...
65 acres belonging to Josiah Riddick adjoining lands of Thomas
Parker, William Arnold and others--sold at instance of Jesse Mathias...
Jno.V.Sumner   K. Ballard

75 3 Aug 1829--James R. Riddick, sheriff, to John A. Anderson and
Abraham Cross of Hertford...$100...150 acres belonging to Peter
Boss to cover debts; first tract of 100 acres adjoins Abraham Cross,
Richard Odom and others and last tract of 50 acres adjoins lands
of Samuel Brown, George Brooks and others...
                                              J.R. Riddick

76 20 Aug 1828--John P. Hudgins to John R. Felton...$79...Negro
girl, Lucinda...
                                     John P. Hudgins

76 20 Aug 1828--John Eure Sr. to Nathan Smith...$30...6 acres be-
ginning at ash a corner tree in Little Cypress Swamp Joseph Smith's
corner now said Nathan's running up swamp to a neck of sourwood to
a dogwood to Great Cypress Swamp to Joseph Smiths corner across
ridge...   John(x)Eure
Mills Eure
Thomas Smith

77 21 Aug 1828--Joel Hudgins to Jesse Hudgins...$2250...151½ acres
N side of main road where he lives beginning at white oak at 6-ft.
ditch a line between Micajah Riddick's heirs and said Joel running
to main road and along road to corner tree between Joel and William
Hudgins...   Joel Hudgins
Mathew M. Dyes
Louisa Pugh

26 Jul 1821--Kedar Ballard, sheriff, to Purnel King...$27...lands
of Alse Green...   K. Ballard
Demsy Vann
Ethel'd Mathews

78 15 Feb 1829--James R. Riddick and wife, Louisa, to John Saunders
$355...88 acres beginning at pine in Isaac Pipkin's line a corner
on said John's NE to small sassafras of Henrietta Copeland's cor-
ner SE to gum in Peter's Swamp down swamp to holly in front of
Saunders house and SW...   J.R. Riddick
Wm. W. Riddick   Louisa Riddick
Mills Riddick

79 23 Aug 1828--James Simpson and wife, Penelope, to Henry G. Will-
iams...$100...41 acres whereon they live bounded on N by lands of
Hillory Willey, E by Levin Cuff on S by Kicheon Norfleet and W by
Miles Parker...   James Simpson
                                            Penelope(x)Simpson
James Parker
Mary Parker

80 5 May 1829--John V. Sumner, sheriff, to Henry Gilliam as agent
for Lemuel C. Moore of Pasquotank by Fieri Facias writ from court
of Camden against Alfred H. Trotman, dec....$50...93½ acres adjoining
lands of Abel Rogerson and James Brinkley and bounded by lands of
Milton Eason, Catherine Creek Swamp and Joseph Hurdle...

W. Hudgins   Jno. V. Sumner
Jno. Beeman

82 3 Jul 1828--Mary Felton to Jethro Riddick...$12...1 acre on main
road leading from courthouse to Edenton beginning at stake, a corner
of Frederick Pearce's line running NE to corner of said Mary and W
to line of blazed trees...

                                                  Mary(x)Felton
Jno. Walton
John E. Rawls

82 29 Nov 1828--William Eure to son, Thomas, plantation whereon
he lives...10 acres to be run out of that is to be divided to him
and his brother, Thomas, who is to have other half...

                                                  William(x)Eure
Purnal King
Elisha Eure
Samuel Eure

82 27 Nov 1827--Hardy Eason and Charles Eason...$12.50...12½ acres
it being his part of pecosin land that he heired in division of his
father, Frederick Eason, dec. real estate and is No. 3...

                                                  Hardy(x)Eason
Jos. Gordon

82 17 Jul 1829--Whitmill Stallings to David Outlaw...$400...160
acres on S side of Catherine Creek Swamp joining lands of Peter B.
Minton, John Mitchell, Thomas Hobbs and said Stallings and others,
formerly known by name of M. Roundtree's tract...

                                              Whitmill Stallings
John B. Walton
Simon Walters

84 28 Jul 1829--Wills Cowper of borough of Norfolk to James Harrell
of town of Suffolk...$3875 acres known by name Sunsbury whereon he
formerly resided and includes 600 acres: 401 sold by Josiah Collins,
dec. to John Cowper, dec; 24 acres patented by Wills Cowper lying
between last mentioned tract and land belonging to Ed. R. Hunter;
175 acres on E side of Bennetts Creek purchased by said Wills of
James Barnes, dec. adjoining first tract and beginning at Mill Race
of Isaac R. Hunter up creek to Hinton's land to main public road
to Hunter's Mill W to Bennetts Creek E to heirs of Isaac Hunter,dec.

William B. Whitehead   Wills Cowper
Noah Felton
James A. Riddick

85 18 Aug 1829--James Harrell of Suffolk to James Coston...$3500

plantation called Sunsbury and containing 600 acres...

James Harrell

George Costen
Will. C. Brooks

86 18 Dec 1828--Mary Miller to Nancy Miller...$100...40 acres and
is one undivided half of land Robert Miller died possessed of, joining lands of John C. Gordon, Richard H. Ballard and others...

Mary Miller

Jno. C. Gordon
Mary Hunter

87 10 Jul 1829--Henry E. Blanchard to Benbury Walton...$60...30
acres beginning at red oak a corner of said Waltons in Joseph Sut-
ton's line S to a pine a corner of Robert Blanchards and NE to corner of said Benbury...

Henry E. Blanchard

W. Hays
R. Mathews

87 4 Dec 1827--Benjamin Blanchard to William Blanchard...$50...50
acres beginning at a stake a corner between dwelling house running
a direct line through to William Pearce's corner at a sassafras to
a path near Meeting House...

B. Blanchard

William Hofler
Frederick Blanchard

88 17 Aug 1829--James King to John King...$75...37½ acres, his half
of land conveyed to said James and John by their aunt, Alse Green,
by deed of gift--on Lickingroot Branch beginning at a pine a corner
in Ann Harrell's line to a white oak a corner of Jethro Eure's line
and back to branch...

James King

Jno.D.Pipkin
Job R.Hall

88 5 Aug 1829--Elisha Keen of Hertford to Benjamin Eure...$65...70
acres beginning at black gum in Panther Swamp a corner of William
Harrells and Mills Eure along Harrells line to a maple a corner of
said William and Jethro Harrell to Cypress Pond and back to Eures...

Elisha(x)Keen

Seth Tebout
Redic(x)Eure

89 25 May 1829--Abraham Harrell to William Arnold...$350...103
acres beginning at Thomas W. Ballards corner on main road leading
from Edenton to Suffolk W to land belonging to heirs of John Brothers, dec. S to main road and N...

A. Harrell

Wm.W.Stedman
Ethel'd Mathews

89 21 Mar 1829--Uriah Eure of Gates County and Lewis Eure of Hertford County to friend, Boon Eure...33 acres beginning at corner
pine of John Beemans to hickory in Thomas Hoggards line to a white
oak a corner of Abram W. Parker's, along Parkers line N to a pine

in Parkers line W to corner pine in David Lewis line S to corner
red oak in Uriah Eure's gap W along path to a pine between said
Uriah and Bray Eures fence...Uriah and Nancy Eure to live on said
land during natural lives...

Abrm.W.Parker
Nathan(H)Harrell

Uriah Eure
Lewis Eure

90 26 June 1828--Augustus Morgan of Suffolk to John F. Hays, resid-
ing in Mathews Co., Va...$500...10 acres near courthouse on E side
of road joining Thomas Saunders, John Mathews and John D. Pipkin...

Augustus Morgan

James M. Bailey
Jno.W.Parker

91 25 May 1829--Abram Harrell to Thomas W. Ballard...$450...200
acres beginning at small red oak on road leading from Suffolk to
Edenton a corner of said Abrams along road to Jason Franklins line
NW to lightwood stump to state line to Abram Riddicks line of marked
trees W to a pine corner of John Brothers and SE to a stake in an old
path...

A. Harrell

Wm. W. Stedman
Ethel'd Matthews

91 7 Nov 1829--John V. Sumner to Benjamin B. Ballard...$5.00 to se-
cure to Jethro Sumner against payment of note of $1766.43 executed
to David Benton 25 Apr 1826 and one to John Roberts for $715.11...
plantation on NE side of Bennetts Creek adjoining lands of heirs
of John Riddick, dec., Moses Speight and others...and Negroes Eason,
Giles, Isaac, Jack, Joe, Willis, Stephen, Charles, George, Nelson,
Miles, John, Peggy, Pheba, Rosa, Tom, Amy, Mary, Little Joe, Little
Mary, Armica, Phillis, and Betty; all household and kitchen furniture, 4 horses, 2 mules and all stock of cattle, hogs and sheep with
all crops of corn and fodder...

John V. Sumner
B.B. Ballard
I. Sumner

Jno. Gary
Thos. Gary

93 14 Nov 1829--Etheldred Mathews to Joseph Gordon...$1.00 to
secure to David Benton two notes: one for $285.19 and one for
$2514 ...307 acres where he lives, brandy still, sorrell mare,
apple mill, mare and colt, cart and wheels, 2 yoke of steers,
cart and wheels, 6 head cattle, 11 head of sheep, 32 hogs, 4 beds
and furniture, 6 windsor chairs, 8 flags, 1 walnut table, 2 pails,
40 barrels of corn, 2000 barrels of fodder, 1 trunk,2 pine tables,
1 bofat, crockery ware, 1 pine chest, 1 dest, parcel of books,3
iron pots, oven, grill and gridiron, 2 water tubs, 1 chest, 2
brass candle sticks, 2 pair fire tongs, 1 shovel, 1 looking glass,
2 sets knives and forks, Negro men Noah and Charles...

Ethel'd Mathews
David(x)Benton
Jos. Gordon

Kedar Ballard
D. Godwin

94 19 Nov 1829--Abram Harrell to Nathan Cullens, Moses B. Harrell,
John V. Sumner and Whitmill Stallings, trustees, to secure debt

of $520 to said Sumners endorsed to Thomas Twine and to dis-
charge duties of Abram Harrell as guardian of Elizabeth and Cena
Eason...sell to Whitmill Stallings 232½ acres being tract whereon
he lives adjoining lands of Andrew Harrell, John Alpin and others...

A. Harrell
Aug. Moore

95 22 Feb 1826--Joseph Gwin and wife, Elizabeth, of Jones County,
Ga. to Henry G. Williams...$140...tract of land which Elizabeth
inherited as heir of Demsey Williams, dec. in last will of Jonathan Williams and adjoining lands of Levi Creecy, Hillory Willey, Levi
Rogers and others...   Joseph(x)Gwin
Nicholas W. Wells   Elizabeth(x)Gwin
     Charles J. McDonald was judge of Georgia Court and deed was
attested to by Daniel Newman, secretary of state.

96 29 Apr 1828--Nancy Williams of Jones County, Ga. to Henry G.
Williams...$100...land which she inherited as heir of Demsey Will-
iams, dec. in last will of Jonathan Williams and which joins lands
of Levi Creesy, Hillory Willey, Levi Rogers and others...
                                                  Nancy(+)Williams
Stephen Renfro
     O.H. Kenans was judge of Georgia Court and E. Hamilton was sec-
retary of state.

     97 1 Apr 1830--Mills Riddick, John Gatling and Riddick Gatling
bound to John Owen, governor, in $10,000 bound for Mills Riddick as
clerk and master of court of equity for Gates County...
                                                  Mills Riddick
                                                  John Gatling
                                                  R. Gatling

98 14 Jan 1830--Abel Rogerson to Robert Riddick $1.00...137 acres
whereon he lives adjoining lands of Jasper Trotman, Joseph Hurdle
and others and Negro woman, Charlotte and boy, Henry; and to secure
to Henry Gilliam and Nathan Riddick notes to James Lassiter for
$216.66 and Joseph Freeman for $210.06...
                                                  Abel Rogerson
Joseph Trotman   H. Gilliam
Henry King   Nathan Riddick
                                                  Ro. Riddick
100 5 Oct 1829--James Brown to Jesse Brown...$125...
49 acres beginning at red oak a corner tree between John and James
Brown along Gilliams line to Sally Brown to corner tree of William
Pilands...   James(x)Brown

Jno. Beeman
D. Parker

100 16 Nov 1829--Frederick Blanchard and wife, Nancy, to Mary
Hudgins...$10...6 acres adjoining said Mary and formerly belong-
ing to Sally Blanchard; it being a part held by Amariah Blanchard Jr., dec. from his father, Amariah Blanchard Sr. and being
share drawn by Nancy in division of her brother, Amariah Jr...
                                                  Frederick Blanchard
Timothy Walton   Nancy(x)Blanchard
Job(x)Blanchard

101 1 Feb 1830--James R. Riddick, sheriff, to Joseph Gordon...
$250 and further sum of $10...to comply with writ in favor of
John Roberts against Abraham Harrell and Joseph Gordon...230½
acre plantation whereon said Abraham lives and 290 acres whereon
said Moses B. lives, being plantation whereon Moses Briggs formerly lived and which was devised by said Briggs to Abraham Harrell
and wife for life and after their death to Moses B. Harrell; first
tract adjoins lands of John Alpin and Andrew Harrell and second
tract adjoins lands of Joseph Riddick, William Harrell and others...
                                                    J.R. Riddick
Jesse Wilson

102 15 Feb 1828--Division of real estate of Jesse Wilson, dec.
Survey No. 1--Mary Hunter...372 acres beginning at two populars
at dividing line near Middle Branch to middle of lane along lane
N to a persimmon tree E to large pine SE to Jesse Eason's corner
in Thomas Hunter's line SW to forked pine in Elisha Hunters and to
head of Middle Branch to a cypress and down branch. No. 2--Henry
Lassiter and wife...491 acres beginning at mouth of Wolf Pit Branch
at black gum then NE to road to white oak SE to persimmon tree to
Jacob Hunters new survey S to David Rice's corner tree near Great
Marsh along Rice's line to Jesse Easons SW to Thomas Hunter's line
NW to large pine...to Middle Branch NW to Meherrin Swamp...
                                                    Jos. Gordon
                                                    Robert Hill
                                                    E.R. Hunter
                                                    I.R. Hunter

104 1 Nov 1823--Division of real estate of Riddick Trotman: Survey
No. 1--Agatha--45 acres beginning at mouth of Poly Branch up run
to corner of Ezekiel Trotman's SE along his line to cypress on edge
of Catherine Creek. No. 2--Ezekiel--32 acres beginning at small post
oak a corner of Agatha's in Alexander Freeman's line NE to Moses
Trotmans to Catherine Creek and down creek. No. 3--Moses--48 acres
beginning at pine at Ezekiels corner in Freeman's line N to small
persimmon tree to a pine on side of Frederick's Mill Pond down side
to mouth of gutt that empties into pond and SE to Mill Race to
Catherine Creek and to bridge. No. 4--Penninah--27 acres beginning
at sweet gum in James Baker's line at Catherine Creek Swamp NE to
main road that leads from Muddy Cross to Sandy Cross NE to middle
of lane that leads to house SE near old dam to Bakers. No. 5--
Elisha--27 acres beginning in main road at Penninah's corner along
dividing line to cypress to old dam down swamp to Joseph Hurdle's
line to main road. No. 6--Riddick--21 acres beginning at main road
at Penninah's corner NE to a small pine near a dead oak supposed
to be in James Brinkleys line E to two post oaks in Brinkleys line
on main road and SW along road...
                                                    Jno.T.Benton
Agatha to pay Riddick $92   Nathan Riddick
Ezekiel to pay Penninah $43   John Hoffler
Moses to pay Elisha $14
105 28 Jun 1828--Division of estate of Abner Lassiter Sr.: Survey
No. 1--Kadah Lassiter...4 acres 2 roods beginning at a pine corner
of Abner Pearces in Richard Bond's heirs line along old path SW to

Deep Gutt to a swamp gum a corner of Kicheon Howell's NE and also
11 acres of Aaron Lassiter's tract beginning at a pine on edge of
old road a corner of Kedah's. No. 2--Kicheon Howell in right of wife,
Easter...13 acres beginning at sweet gum corner of Kadah's at Deep
Gutt to water oak a corner of Abner Lassiters. No. 3--Abner...13
acres 2 roods beginning at white water oak a corner in said Howell's
in Deep Gutt along Pearce's line NE to post oak near path N to maple
NW to pine to Howell's line...

Willis I. Riddick
Jas. W. Riddick
Tim. Walton
Abner Pearce

106 8 Nov 1825--Division of land of Robert Parker: Survey No. 1--
Children of Abraham Parker (Nancy, Henry, Robert and Charity)...24
acres beginning at bridge in road leading from courthouse to Suffolk
SW to a pine to John D. Pipkin's line and up branch. No. 2--Richard
Parker...24 acres beginning at pine in road SW to corner of Nancy
Bond's to stake in field. No. 3--William Parker...24 acres begin-
ning at a popular a corner in Pipkin Branch SW to stake in old field
and SE up branch. No. 4--Children of Jesse Parker (Sophia, Penny,
Lidia, Thursa and Mary)...24 acres beginning at stake in corner of
No. 1 SW to water oak down to dividing line and W. No. 5--Sally
Parker...24 acres beginning at black gum in branch in Pipkin's line
SW to stake in old field to run of branch. No. 6--Children of Willis
Parker (Nancy Bond and Mary Craper) 24 acres beginning at small pine
near a larger one at dividing line SW to edge of creek and NE. No 7--
James Brown and others. Children of Christian Brown (Mary Evans,
Nancy Lassiter, Willis Brown, Eliza Parker, James Brown, Betsey and
Louisa Parker)...24 acres beginning at large cypress a corner of No.
9 in creek swamp SW to a pine to run of branch. No. 8--Jane Brown...
24 acres beginning at pine a corner at edge of creek to small cypress
to creek that empties into Bennetts Creek. No. 9--Elizabeth Bullock...
24 acres beginning at black gum near creek along dividing line to edge
of creek. No. 10--Priscilla Hays...24 acres beginning at small cypress
in dividing line across an island along creek swamp to run of branch
to black gum at old land.

Wm.W.Riddick
James Williams
Pryor Savage

109 24 Jan 1828--Division of land of Simeon and David Brinkley:
No. 1--Simeon Brinkley's heirs...298 acres beginning at cypress on
S side of Orapeak Swamp a corner on Fountaine's heirs to corner of
David Brinkley SE to Richard H. Ballard's along a ditch a dividing
line and NW. No. 2--David Brinkley...298 acres beginning at gum in
Orapeak Swamp NE to corner on Miles Brinkleys SW and then N to a
corner of Col. Josiah Riddicks NE to cypress and SE to corner of
Simeon Brinkleys...

Jno.C.Gordon
Wm.W.Stedman
T.W.Carr

111 17 May 1824--Division of land of James Gatling: No. 1--William
Gatling...257 acres, the Home Tract, beginning at a pine a corner of

Susan Boush SE to black gum in run of Mills Swamp up swamp to Isaac
Pipkin's Mill house to Etheldred B. Gatling's corner NE to small
branch and then NW to a red oak, head of branch to John Saunders
corner and SW... No. 2--Dr. John Gatling...274 acres, the Speight
Tract, beginning at small ash a corner of Susan Boush and in Eff
Lewis line then NW to a white oak to a sweet gum a corner of Eff
Lewis and Ira Odom due N and then NW to Manney's Ferry and along
road... No. 3--Charles E. Sumners in right of wife, Martha...400
acres, the Old Place, beginning at sweet gum a corner on Exum Lewis
SW and then SE to a maple a corner of Exum Lewis and Isaac Pipkin
and then SW to Wynns and Jones corner...to a white oak to a small
pine, Sparkman's corner, to Carters tract and NE to a sweet gum a
corner on Kiddy Lewis and William Jordon and in head of small branch
and along branch... No. 4--Riddick Gatling...323 acres, the Carter
Tract, and 42 acres, the William Gatling Tract, beginning at sweet gum
a corner on Old Place SW to corner of Sparkmans to red oak at the
Doctor's old road along road to a red oak a corner on Parkers NE
to heirs of Col. William Goodman then SW. The William Gatling Tract
begins at pine corner of Susan Boush SW to Speight's Branch to
Manney's Ferry Road and along road... No.5 --Ann Gatling...447½
acres...6 small tracts: Elizabeth Lewis, Judah, Flax Island, Sand
Banks, Rogers Pocosin and 48-acre tract on Winton Road...beginning in
Mill Swamp to Isaac Pipkins corner to Pryer Savages corner in Wet
Slash...to Odom's estate to Chowan Rivers near upper end of Rochells
Fishery to James Hare's corner in Speight's Old Mill Pond across
Sand Banks NW to river pocosin and 2 acres at Gut Landing on Chowan
River ...to Henry Copelands line SE to William Goodmans. William to
pay Riddick $129.11 and Charles E. Sumners to pay Riddick $7.23
and John $179.09.

Isaac Pipkin
H. Willey
William Goodman
Wm.M.Harvey
Lem'l Goodman

113 Feb Ct 1827--Division of estate of Nathaniel Pruden: Survey
No. 1--William D. Pruden...47 acres beginning at a beech a corner
of Celia M. Pruden's and David Riddick SE to gum in Muddy Swamp
and down swamp to Abram Morgans. No. 2--Celia M. Pruden...64 acres
3 roods beginning at pine stump a corner of Lewis W. Pruden's SW
along David Riddick's line to a beach...NE to forked red oak a
corner of Seth Benton's and NW. No. 3--Lewis W. Pruden...71 acres 3
roods beginning at pine stump corner of said Celia's and Riddicks
to Benton's line to corner of Moses S. Newsome's to Riddicks field.
No. 4--Moses B. Newsome in right of wife, Martha E...50 acres beginning at corner of Charles Prudens and said Riddick's line SE to
Abram C. Morgans. No. 5--Charles N. Pruden...50 acres beginning at
water oak in Newsome and Morgan's corner NE to Sarah Arnolds and NW.

George Kittrell   Henry Pugh
David Riddick   Benbury Walton
William Hudgins   Joel Hudgins

114 10 Aug 1829--Division of land of Richard Bond: Survey No. 1--
Noah Bond...10 acres beginning at sweet gum SE to beach and NE

along a line of marked trees. No. 2--Milly Bond...10 acres beginning at a sweet gum NE to a persimmon tree and SW. No. 3--Samuel S.
Bond...10 acres beginning at sweet gum NW along line of marked
trees. No. 4--Richard Bond...10 acres beginning at a pine NW to
beach and SE. No. 5--Nancy Bond...20 acres on Deep Gut beginning
at gum to Kiddy Hare's line binding on heirs of James Costen to
a pine in old road and includes an island in Norfleet's Mill Pond
of 7 acres. No. 6--William Bond...23 acres beginning at popular
corner NE to mill pond and NW. No. 7-- Alsey Bond...23 acres beginning at peach tree down dividing line NE and S to apple tree.
No. 8--Eliza Bond...23 acres beginning at peach tree SE to dividing line. No. 9--Margaret Bond...23 acres beginning at pine tree
and along dividing line SE. No. 10--Henry Bond...23 acres beginning at pine and along dividing line SE. No. 11--Sally Bond...23
acres beginning at dividing line NW. No. 2 to pay $4.21¼ to Nos.
6,7,8,9,10 and 11; to No. 1 $14.34¼; to No. 3 $9.34¼ and to No. 5
$11.68½.

                                        J. Walton
                                        David Parker
                                        Willis J.Riddick
                                        James Costen

115 10 Aug 1829--Moses B. Harrell to James P. Small...$1.00 and
to make safe to Riddick Hunter and Andrew R. Harrell security for
$20 note to Jesse Brown; $40 or $50 to Thomas Twine and one to
Andrew Harrell...3 head horses, 29 hogs, 10 sheep, 1 yoke oxen,
cart and wheels, bed, household and kitchen furniture...
                                        M.B. Harrell
John Voight   Jas. P. Small
Jas.(x)Davis   Riddick Hunter
                                        Andrew R. Harrell
116 14 Dec 1829--Moses B. Harrell to John W. Harrell...$1500...
250 acres whereon he lives...
                                        Moses B. Harrell
Noah Hurdle
William Harrell
116
116 7 Dec 1829--M.B. Harrell to John W. Harrell...$1600...Negroes
Julia and children, Wells, Fanny, Jen, Louveasor and Julia; Lucea
and children Dinah and Willis and Negro woman Hanna...
                                        M.B. Harrell
A. Harrell
Noah Hurdle

116 1 Jan 1830--A. Harrell to John W. Harrell...$175...Negroes
Sam and Samboe...   A. Harrell
Ethel'd Mathews
M.B. Harrell

117 26 Nov 1829--Jacob Odom to Isaac Speight...$200...123 acres
beginning at corner pine of David Cross and others in Pine Swamp
running James Brady's line to Burwell Griffith's corner and along
his line to Abraham Cross to Crawfords and up swamp..Jacob Odom

Abraham Smith

117 14 Aug 1829--Armetia Brinkley and her husband, Riddick Jones,
to Jesse Mathias...$500...30 acres joining said Mathias, Demsey Vann
and others...6 Negroes Any and 3 children, Jacob and Hanah, all stock,
cart and wheels and all household furniture...

                                          Armetia(x)Brinkley
                                          Riddick Jones
Jethro Brinkley
Benjamin Brinkley

117 2 Nov 1829--John Blanchard Sr. to Mary Hudgins...$12...42½
acres on main road from courthouse to Edenton...it being a part of
plantation whereon his father, Amariah Blanchard, formerly lived and
died and deeded to said John Sr...beginning at chinquepin tree, formerly corner of Thomas Blanchards and running SE to high water mark
in Beaverdam Swamp to Mill Pond to persimmon tree at mouth of Mirey
Branch and up branch...   John Blanchard
Maria Elliott
Tim. Walton

118 23 Apr 1829--John V. Sumner, sheriff, to Walton Freeman...$200
plus $14.95 in interest and costs...land belonging to Frederick
Blanchard...sold by court writ...
                                          Jno.V.Sumner

119 19 Nov 1829--David Outlaw to Henry Bond...$200...Negro Dinah
and certain tract of land to secure deed of trust given by Frederick and Reuben Hinton with Peter B. Minton as trustee...
                                          Jno.V.Sumner
J. Riddick
Nathan Cullens

120 18 Aug 1829--Jno.V. Sumner,sheriff, to Miles Parker...$535.50...
530 acres of land belonging to John Saunders adjoining lands of
Riddick Gatling, William Gatling, John Speight and others...sold by
court writ in favor of Peyton Lynch...
                                          Jno.V.Sumner

121 27 Oct 1829--William Hudgins to John V. Sumner...$250...150
acres beginning at main road leading from John Mathews to court-
house at a corner dogwood in Mathew Dye's line and along his line
E and S to William Cleaves line to a corner of Thomas Riddicks to
Mills Williams...   William Hudgins
Ben.B.Ballard
Reuben Brothers

122 13 Nov 1829--Benjamin Brinkley to Jesse Mathias...$350.54...
Negroes Abram, Peter and Lewis...
                                          Benjamin Brinkley
Ro. Riddick
B.B.Ballard

122 17 Nov 1829--John C. Gordon to Noah Speight...$4...½ acre be-
ginning on W side of road leading from Folly to Hertford and running
road to Speight's line to William Miller's line...
                                          John C. Gordon
Open Court

122 30 Apr 1828--Nathaniel Doughtie to John H. Haslett...$175...
Negro boy Henry...
                                          Nathaniel Doughtie
Open Court

122 17 May 1830--Jethro Sumner, Joseph Gordon and Jethro H. Riddick
are bound to John Owen, Esq., Gov. for 2000 pds...
Henry Pugh   J. Sumner
Wm.C.Cowper   Jos Gordon
R. Gatling   Jeth. Riddick

123 14 Aug 1830--James R. Riddick, sheriff, to Abram W. Parker...
$61...130 acres belonging to Elisha Eure whereon Demsey Parker now
lives beginning at run of swamp in Fort Island Road to a corner pine
in John Sparkman's line along his line to corner oak S and E to David
Lewis line and along his line to road and up swamp...Sold by court
order to cover notes of $25.64 and $34.06 to Miles Parker and one for
$72.60 to Demsey Eure made by Elisha Eure...
                                          J.R. Riddick
T. Saunders
Myles Parker

124 17 Aug 1830--Abram W. Parker to Demsey Parker...$61.25...130
acres beginning at run of big swamp in Fort Island to corner pine
in John Sparkmans line to David Lewis line to road leading from
courthouse to Winton across road and up swamp...land bought at sheriff
sale and formerly belonging to Elisha Eure...
                                          Abrm. W. Parker
Jesse Brown
I. Brown

125 15 Sep 1829--Thomas Smith to James Smith...$25...50 acres in
Little Cypress Swamp which descended to him from his mother, Mary
Smith at her death, beginning at black gum in John Eure's line to
Saunders Carters to a corner tree in Reuben Parker's line to a pine
a corner tree in Abraham Beeman's line in head of Hawtree Branch and
down run of swamp...
                                          Thomas Smith
Kicheon Taylor
John(x)Powell

126 26 Oct 1829--Robert Riddick (of Micajah) to son, Henry...$100
Negro girl Emma 9 years old...
                                          Robert Riddick
John Gordon
James Briggs

126 26 Oct 1829--Isaac R. Hunter to Henry Riddick...$50...6 acres
beginning on E side of main road from Suffolk to Edenton at a large
ditch which crosses road and which is N boundry between said parties
and up road S and then W...
                                          I.R. Hunter
John Gordon
W. Hull

126 8 Jan 1829--Chowan: Burton Hathaway of Tyrell appoints Wm.D.
Rascoe of Edenton as his attorney to convey Negro man, Tom, who was
devised to him by Richard Mitchell...
                                          B. Hathaway
Wm.F.B.Bennett

127 6 Jan 1830--Willis H. and Andrew B. Woodley, executors of Andrew
Woodley, dec. of Isle of Wight, to Kicheon Norfleet...$37.50...150
acres of swamp land, which formerly belonged to Dr. Willis Woodley,
dec. and was sold by a sheriff's sale in which Andrew B. Woodley
became purchaser...beginning at line of Thomas Sumners, dec. , the
upper line between Sumners and Timothy Lassiter on Bennetts Creek
to Richard Bond's line to end of Bond's land, an island above mouth
of Watery Swamp NW up run of Bennetts Creek...

W. H.Woodley
Andrew B.Woodley

Jno.P.Thomas
Jno.R.Norfleet
Robt.W.Gibbs

128 10 Jan 1830--Kicheon Norfleet to John R. Norfleet...$19...the
above tract of land...

Kicheon Norfleet

Open Court

128 17 Sep 1830--Elisha Robertson to Garrett Hofler...$1.00...to
insure to John Hinton Sr. and William Hinton, who became security
for $161 bond to John Roberts, and 117 acres of land adjoining
lands of John Morris, Lavinia Parker, Henry B. Lassiter and John
Roberts. Also 40 barrells corn 2 feather beds and bedsteads furniture 7 head of sheep 4 head hogs 3 head of cattle 2000 weight blade
fodder 1 loom and gear household and kitchen furniture crop of peas
1 horse and cart farm utensils working tools and 3 sides of leather...

Elisha(x)Robertson
G. Hofler
John Hinton
William Hinton

Henry B. Lassiter
Clement Hill

130 30 Aug 1828--J. Waddle to Tilly W. Carr...$250...400 acres of
juniper timber on pecosin land belonging to his ward, Charles Skinner,
for 6 years...

J. Waddle

Abrm.Cross

130 1 Sep 1828--T.W. Carr to Dr. Isaac Pipkin...$25...½right in
juniper swamp purchase of John Waddle as guardian of Charles Shinner
for timber for 6 years...

T.W.Carr

Abrm.Cross

131 16 Aug 1825--William W. Riddick, sheriff, to Joseph Riddick...
$29.97...land belonging to Jethro W. Sumner, dec. on N side of Ben-
netts Creek bounded by lands of James Figg, John Figg, Thomas Riddick, Kicheon Norfleet and others...sold by court writ at instance
of Thomas Riddick...

Wm.W.Riddick

Law.S.Daughtry
Kindred Parker

132 28 May 1830--Theophelus White to George Costen...$1.00...all
his crop of corn peas and to insure note of $25.40 to Thomas Twine...

Theophelus White
George Costen

Elisha H. Hunter

133 30 May 1827--John Blanchard to William Blanchard Jr....to insure notes to Benjamin Blanchard for $14.27; William Walton for
$60.96 , $16.85 and $21.72; Henry Gilliam for $55.80 and to John
Walton as guardian of heirs of Riddick Trotman, dec. for $154.26
...100 acres of land whereon John lives joining land of Henry
Walton and Miles Brown, and 3 feather beds and furniture, 3 chests,
2 tables, 1 iron pot, 1 dutch oven, 1 fry pan, tub and pail, 3 pewter basins, 6 pewter plats, 12 spoons, 1 loom and gear, 1 mare and
colt, 1 yound mare, 1 briddle and saddle, 1 riding chear and gear,
1 cart and wheels, 1 brandy still, 6 head of cattle, 10 head of hogs,
20 cider hogshead, 20 cider barrells, 8 geese.

B. Blanchard Jr.   John Blanchard

134 23 Feb 1829--Tilly W. Carr to Kedar Taylor...$37...7 1/10 acres
bounded on S by Thicket Road past Taylors house, on E by land owned
by Jordon Parker and on N by Taylors land known by name Ketty Ralph
Place...
                                                      T.W. Carr
John Benton
John Taylor

135 19 Jan 1829--Micajah Blanchard of Chowan to John Walton...$120...
Negro woman, Leah, 46 years old and girl, Mary, 6 years old...
                                                  Micajah Blanchard

135 16 Apr 1829--John V. Sumner, sheriff, to Walton Freeman...3 tracts
of land belonging to heirs of Timothy Freeman, dec. sold by court writs
in favor of John Roberts, Josiah Coffield and Whitmill Stallings and
Andrew Baker. First tract of 150 acres for $500 where said Timothy
formerly lived adjoining lands of Timothy Walton, William Blanchard
and others. Second tract of 156 acres for $420 joining Andrew Baker
and third tract of grist mill and land for $197.50.
                                                    Jno.V.Sumner
Henry W. Skinner
James Boothe

136 30 Oct 1829--Moses Speight to Edward R. Hunter...$155...50 acres
beginning at pine in Thomas Eason's line thence an E course to post
oak a corner tree between heirs of John Riddick and said Speight N
by line of marked trees to Riddick and Sumners line and W to creek...
                                                  Moses(x)Speight
Bn.B.Ballard
L.E.Hunter

137 2 Nov 1829--Edward R. Hunter to Isaac R. Hunter...$700...50
acres beginning at red oak at fork of road W to a branch down branch
E to main road from Suffolk to Edenton...   E.R.Hunter
Henry Riddick
William Hall

137 6 Sep 1829--Jesse Hudgins to Noah Harrell...$1600...187 acres
on S side of main road that leads from place where Humphrey Hudgins

formerly lived beginning at forks of road near John Mathews binding
on road S and then E to a branch to Josiah Hudgins heirs...

Jesse Hudgins

Jas.C.Riddick
David Parker

138 17 Nov 1829--Noah Harrell to Abraham Beeman, Esq. $1500...187
acres of land. (Same as described above).

Noah Harrell

Wm.L.Boothe
Zaccra Hays

139 28 Jul 1829--Solloman Roundtree to Henry Gilliam...$1.00 and
payment of $367.46 note to Daughtry and Webb...56 acres of land
adjoining Isaac Pipkin, Benjamin Hayes and others and Negro man,
Isaac...

Soloman Roundtree

Lem.G.Darden
Law.L.Daughtry

Daughtry & Webb
H. Gilliam

139 16 Nov 1829--Jesse Wiggens to Wilie Riddick...$150...70 acres
formerly belonging to Robert Parker and heirs of James Parker, dec.
beginning at gum along Bentons line to a maple on edge of Gum Branch,
a corner of said Riddick, Benton and Wiggens and along their lines...

Jesse Wiggens

D. Parker
John B. Walton

140 16 Feb 1829--Barnes Goodman to Jethro Willey...$281.50...Negro
man Enos and for deed in trust given to him by Nathaniel Doughtie
to secure to Charles E. Sumner for debts to John Willey...

Barnes Goodman

Henry Willey
George W. Smith

141 4 Jun 1829--John D. Pipkin to George Kittrell, Benbury Walton,
John O. Hunter, Reuben Harrell, Abram Beeman, Reuben Hinton, Jesse
Brown, James Smith and John B. Harrell, trustees in trust...$40...
½ acres land to build house of worship for Methodist Episcopal Church
of USA...beginning at white oak stump on W side of main road a corner to Abram Parkers W and NW along Pipkins line...

Jno.D.Pipkin

H. Gilliam
W.G. Daughtry

143 11 Apr 1829--William Baker to James Baker...$150...27 acres land
adjoining land of heirs of Elisha Trotman, Riddick Trotman and James
Roundtree...

W. Baker

Abraham Twine
Treacy(x)Gwin

143 28 Mar 1829--Uriah Eure to son, Bray...two pieces of land. The
first of 25 acres begins at a corner pine of John Beeman's line down
run of Mirey Branch to Cypress Swamp to David Lewis line E to corner
of said Lewis and Boon Eure. The second tract of 15 acres begins at

a pine in Great Marsh to James Piland and Reuben Harrell's up
branch to Sarum Creek Road...

Uria_h(x)Eure

Abrm.W.Parker
Wm.H.Savage

144 10 Oct 1829--James T. Freeman to Hance Hofler...$360...125 acres
beginning at pine on Mill Swamp running up swamp to Juniper bridge
along his old line to shite oak at head of Poly Branch down branch
and binding on John White's line to a gum a corner tree between heirs
of Riddick Trotman, dec, said White and Thomas L. Spivey...

Jas.T.Freeman

P.B. Minton
H.H. Eure

145 17 Nov 1829--Christian Riddick to David Outlaw...$25...57 acres
beginning at said Outlaw's line (it being her dower of land of Miles
Roundtree, dec.)...

Christian(x)Riddick

Josiah E. Jones
I. Riddick

145 4 Feb 1829--Henry Hunter to Elizabeth Reed...$37.50...his un-
divided right in land formerly belonging to Theopulis Hunter, dec.
bounded by Cloe Lassiter, Abner Pearce and others...

Henry(x)Hunter

M. Roberts
John Roberts

146 29 Jan 1830--Benjamin Blanchard to Henry Bond...$112...land where-
on he lives...

B. Blanchard

Kedar Hinton
James Bond

146 8 Feb 1830--Benjamin Blanchard Jr. to Henry Bond...$100...land
whereon he lives...
B. Blanchard

B.Blanchard

Kedar Hinton

147 8 Feb 1830--Benjamin Blanchard Jr. to Henry Bond...$40...1
sorrell horse and parcel of fodder...

B. Blanchard

Kedar Hinton

147 8 Feb 1830--William Eure to William L. Boothe...$1.00 and to
secure to Exum Lewis and David Parker $10.22½ note...12½ acre plan-
tation whereon he lives, corn crop, 4 head hogs, 1 table and cast pot.

Wm.(x)Eure

Wm.W.Cowper
John Willey

147 12 Nov 1830--Henry B. Lassiter to James T. Freeman...$1.00 and
to secure to Garrett Hofler as trustee for debt to John Roberts...
two tracts of land. The first one in Indian Neck of 30 acres, which
he purchased of Elisha Robertson bound by lands of John Roberts,

Lavinia Parker and said Robertson and main road leading to Parker's Landing. The second tract of 15 acres is part of plantation whereon he lives bounded by Clement Hill's avenue running to Isaac Lassiter's line and across said Henry's land...

J. Walton
Wright Hays

Henry B. Lassiter
Jas. T. Freeman
G. Hofler

149 27 Oct 1830--Henry Pugh to William E. Pugh...$1.00....Negro Man Moses, girl Venus and boy Jim and in consideration for $100 bond given Henry Gilliam and John Roberts...

John Roberts

Henry Pugh
H. Gilliam
Wm.E.Pugh

150 26 Oct 1830--William L. Boothe to Henry Gilliam...$1.00...Negroes Penny, Henry and Isaac and two tracts of land for payment of $79.38 bond to Abram W. Parker. First tract of 34 1/3 acres adjoins John Riddick,Soloman Green and others and second tract of 82 acres in is Hertford adjoining Elisha H. Sharp, Vollentine Turner, Mrs. Daughtry and others...

Abraham Parker

Wm.L.Boothe
Abrm.W.Parker
H. Gilliam

151 16 Feb 1830--John D. Pipkin to John B. Baker...$10...Negroes: Sam, Dinah, Henry, Lucy, Guy, Cherry, Parthenia, Nancy, Louisa, Rossella, Tom, Charles, Mingo, Daniel and Delia, which were conveyed in a deed of trust 4 Oct 1827...
Jesse Wilson

Jno.D.Pipkin

151 13 Feb 1830--Etheldred Mathews to Jethro Sumner...$65...33½ acres bounded by Kedar Ellis, heirs of John Tooley and heirs of Elisha Brinkley, which was sold by court order to make a division between heirs of Arthur Brinkley and bought by Jethro Brinkley... executed in favor of Jno. C. Gordon, executor of Thomas Parker,dec.

Ethel'd Mathews

T.W.Carr
James Morgan

152 9 Dec 1830--Richard Cross to Henry Gilliam...50 cents to secure note of $48.66 to Simons Roundtree...land whereon he lives adjoining main road...

Jas. Barnes
Jno.R.Gilliam

Richard Cross
Simonds Roundtree
H. Gilliam

152 11 Feb 1830--Richard H. Ballard to James Morgan...$1.00 and to make safe to David Benton $400...300 acres of marsh plantation...

R.H. Ballard

Jesse Wiggens
John Wiggens

153 10 Oct 1827--John V. Sumner, sheriff, to Ethel'd Mathews...$65... 33 1/3 acres belonging to Jethro Brinkley and bounded by Kedar Ellis,

John Tooley and heirs of Elisha Brinkley...

Jno.V.Sumner

T.W.Carr
Bn.B.Ballard

154 23 Jul 1829--Benjamin Knight to Demsey Knight...$12...8 acres
beginning at gum in run of Ellum Swamp Demsey Knight's own line S
to white oak to walnut tree in old field W to main road and E...

Benjamin Knight

Elisha Ellis
Enoch Knight

155 30 Dec 1829--Jasper Trotman to Jethro H. Riddick...$180...90
acres all his land known by name Woods Pasture given to him by his
father, Elisha Trotman by will, beginning at Nathan Riddick's line
W to said Jethro's and to Drew Trotman...

Jasper Trotman

Bushrod Riddick
Calvin Brinkley

155 24 Nov 1828--Harrison Banes and Cynthia Brinkley to Lovina Brinkley...$270.50...Negro Rody and her child Pendor...

Harrison Banes
Cynthia Brinkley

Jesse Mathias

156 26 Aug 1823--Peter Piland to Margaret Rowe...$3000...300 acres
beginning at red oak corner tree in Andrew Johnson's line along his
line to Long Branch up branch to Isaac Pipkins to John Gatling's line
to run of Coles Creek to Carter's land to Abraham Blades and up Long
Branch...except dower of his mother, Susanna Piland...

Peter Piland

Wm.W.Cowper
Andrew Johnson

156 5 Dec 1829--J. Sumner, clerk, to Kedar Taylor...$100.50...Negro
woman, Celia, and her child, Milly, belonging to estate of John Hare,
dec. sold by court order...

J. Sumner

J. Walton

157 28 Nov 1829--Milly Walton to Thomas Walton...$300...75 acres
on N side of Catherine Creek Swamp on main road binding on lands of
Hardy Eason and Nathan Cullens...

Milly Walton

W. Walton
Jno. L. Billups

157 11 Feb 1830--James R. Riddick, sheriff, to John Beeman...$1035
158 acres belonging to Jesse and William Hudgens and whereon Humphrey Hudgins, dec. formerly lived sold by court writ at instance of
said Beeman, John Roberts, Jethro Willey, Josiah Coffield and Mary
Goodman. Land joins lands of George Costen, Rissup Rawls, Noah Harrell and others...

J.R. Riddick

T. Saunders
James C. Riddick

158 5 Feb 1828--Richard Cross to Joseph Riddick (of Thomas)...$300
400 acres beginning at run of Bennetts Creek at Pearces line down
creek to Joseph Gordons line to a post oak to John Walton's line
to David Parkers and along his line to Frederick Fields to Abner
Pearces and run of creek...formerly belonged to Bond Menchew...
Jet.H.Riddick   Richard Cross
Jno.D.Pipkin

159 4 May 1826--Etheldred Mathews to William A. Matthews...$325...
20 acres, all the land belonging to Theresa Mathews, widow of Anthony
Mathews, dec. beginning at a pine a corner of Riddick and William A.
Matthews...
                                                 Etheldred Mathews
D. Knight
John Wiggens

160 27 Jan 1829--Shadrack Felton and wife, Susannah, to Soloman
Green, Jr...$21.50...10 3/4 acres beginning at post oak in Demsey
Sparkmans to Felton's line...
                                                 Shadrack Felton
Wm.L.Boothe   Susannah Felton.
John Beeman

160 15 Mar 1830--John Gatling to James W. Riddick...$500...400 acres
called Lassiter Riddick tract, and Negro woman, Margaret, and boys
Joseph and Toney, and girl, Maria...to secure to Riddick Gatling
notes made to John Roberts...

Jas. Riddick   Jno. Gatling
Micajah Riddick   R. Gatling
                                                 Jas.W.Riddick

161 10 Dec 1829--John Gatling and Mills Riddick to John Roberts...
$650...two lots that Mills Riddick purchased from Isaac R. Hunter,
executor of Isaac Hunter Sr., dec. 15 May 1820. One lot on which
M. Riddick's store and warehouse now stan and other lot known as
landing on Bennetts Creek bounded on E by lands of Thomas Saunders
N and W by lands of Henry Gilliam and on S by creek. Each lot con-
tains one acre...
                                                 John Gatling
W.G. Daughtry   Mills Riddick
John Walton

162 24 Jan 1830--Abel Rogerson to Nathan Riddick...$40...land on
right hand side of road from Sandy Cross to Muddy Cross beginning
at white oak in James Brinkley's line...
                                                 Abel Rogerson

Note: Pages 163 and 164 missing (Jonas Hinton to John Walton; Benbury Walton to John E. Rawls)

165 15 Feb 1830--Theophelius Parker and wife, Sidney, to John Mathews
$18...4 acres bounded on E,W and N by lands of said Mathews and on S
by Nancy Bond...
                                                 Theophelus(x)Parker
Jos.J.Barnes   Sidney(x)Parker
E.H.Riddick

166 20 May 1829--John V. Sumner, sheriff, to William Boush...76
cents taxes on 63 acres belonging to Treasy Walton, adjoining lands
of Jacob Hobbs, Amos Hobbs, Jesse Hobbs and James Baker...

Jno.V.Sumner

Miles Briggs
James Briggs

166 13 Feb 1830--Thomas W. Ballard to Richard H. Ballard...$200...
100 acres...

Thomas W.Ballard

William Arnold
James A. Ballard

167 9 Apr 1828--Simonds Roundtree to Mary Eure...$2.97 property of
Samuel Eure Sr. sold by virtue of execution in favor of Jethro Eure..
1 folding table 1 feather bed looking glass 1 cow and yearling...

Simonds Roundtree

Elisha Eure

167 9 Apr 1828--Benjamin Blanchard Jr. to William D. Taylor...$30
2 feather beds, steads and furniture, corn in crib, 13 head hogs in
woods, bridle, saddle and martingale, all household and kitchen furniture, farm utensils, bacon and other provisions...

Benjamin Blanchard

A. Blanchard
Wm.R.Blanchard

168 7 Dec 1829--Joseph Riddick to Jethro H. Riddick...$150.50...
tract of land bought of Jacob Eason beginning at main road leading
from Sandy Cross to Muddy Cross at a stake, a corner of heirs of
Noah Trotman, dec. to said Jethro's line to Nathan Riddicks W to
James Brinkley and S to Trotmans...

J. Riddick

Burwell Brothers
Nathan Ward

168 23 Jan 1830--Thomas Saunders to Jason Saunders of Gates and John
A. March of Nansemond...$489.72...400 acres, all the land given to
him by Laurence Saunders, after death of his wife;(except the land
he sold to Miles Parker)...beginning at corner of said Parker's line
at head of Gaul Bush to Jesse Wiggens line (formerly Sumners) to
corner of Great Marsh down marsh to Chowan River near Stoney Land
to near Copelands Seine Place and to corner in Parkers line near
Ballards Pocosin. Also, another tract formerly belonging to John
Sumners beginning at corner on Cypress Swamp E on Henry Jones line
to Parkers line to Lang's corner snag and along line to swamp...
after death of Martha Parker...

Thomas Saunders

Myles Parker
James Saunders

169 3 Feb 1830--Henry Lee Goodman to William Lee...$150...69 acres
beginning at pine called The Maj. in John March's line NE to Pearce's
Branch up run to gum and W...

Henry L.Goodman

Francis Duke
David Goodman

170 1 Dec 1829--Thomas and Richard Barnes of Hertford to James
Williams...$1000...810 acres adjoining land of and beginning at
corner line of Robert Saunders heirs running their line to line of
said Williams formerly belonging to John Speight to Burwell Griffiths
line to a maple in land purchased of Henry Richardson, formerly
Elisha Williams; to near head of Little Cypress Swamp to land belonging to said Williams, formerly belonging to Henry Copeland, now
dec. to a gum in branch along Elisha Bonds line to land of Ira Odom,
dec. to Kings Land; it being same tract of land whereon Thomas Barnes,
dec. lived and devised in his will to said Thomas and Richard...

Kinsey Jordan
John K. Ransom

Thomas Barnes
Rich'd Barnes

171 2 Nov 1829--Isaac R. Hunter to Edward R. Hunter...$500...two
Negroes Dick and Charles, a boy...

I.R.Hunter

Henry Riddick
William Hall

171 7 Dec 1829--Nathan Ward to Joseph Riddick...$150...56 acres
bought of Joseph Gordon 11 Oct 1825 beginning at Dan'l Riddicks
corner oak on path E to island N along Riddicks line to corner tree
in Soloman Eason's along his line to Isiah Riddick's line to cause-
way then W...

Nathan Ward

Jet.H.Riddick
Burwell Brothers

172 15 Aug 1829--James Gardner of Nansemond to Abram Riddick of
Hertford...$125...92 acres, The Wainoke Ferry Tract, beginning at
post oak at river bank, a corner of Matilda Rawls thence E to a
bay tree in small branch up branch N to state line binding on line
to Blackwater River ...includes ferry and ferry flat...

Benj. Britt
Abram(x)Benton

James(x)Gardner

173 21 Dec 1829--James Smith to Thomas Hoggard...$50...50 acres,
all his interest in undivided land which descended to him by death
of his father and brother, Thomas, which he purchased, beginning
at black gum in Little Cypress Swamp, a corner tree in John Eure
Sr. line on Saunders line to an oak a corner tree in Reuben Parker's
line to a pine a corner in Abraham Beemans Esq. in head of the Hawtree Branch to Little Cypress Swamp...

James Smith

Wm.L.Boothe
Jesse Harrell

174 8 Feb 1830--Benjamin Williams and wife, Peggy, to William Bond
$48...23 acres on S side of Bennetts Creek, being part of land be-
longing to Richard Bond, father of Peggy, which she inherited from
his estate...begins at pine running N to red oak to corner of dividing line with No. 10...it being the low ground of Watery Swamp
and Bennetts Creek...

Benjamin Williams
Peggy(x)Williams

J. Walton
Jas. W. Riddick

175 4 Dec 1829--Henry Riddick and wife, Lydia A., to Elisha Umphlett...$150...100 acres which Rodon Odom purchased of Edward Vann
adjoining lands of Taylor Cross and John Gatling...

H. Gilliam
Elisha H. Bond

Henry Riddick
Lydia A.Riddick

176 15 Jan 1828--Samuel R. Morgan to Abraham Morgan...$96...Negro
man, Sam, and to pay to William Hudgins, administrator of Abraham
C. Morgan, dec. note made 23 Nov 1827...

Samuel R. Morgan

176 4 Mar 1830--Charles and Ira Carter to Jacob Odom...$40...black
mare, Sall...

Richard Odom

Ira(x)Carter
Charles Carter

176 1 Dec 1829--John Hinton Jr. to William Hinton...$400...130 acres
whereon he lives bounded on N and W by prong of Roberts Mill Pond,
which separated it from lands of Charles Felton, dec. and on S and
E by lands of Willis R. Bond and Jacob Powell...

Mills Roberts
Jno.Bond

John Hinton

178 25 Jan 1828--John Roberts to William Hinton...$150...tract of
land formerly belonging to Kedar Hill, beginning at popular in said
William's line running his line to Gabriel's Branch, and being on
E side of Roberts Mill Pond...

Mills Roberts

John Roberts

178 3 Dec a827--James Powell to William Hinton...$200...75 acres
whereon he lives adjoining lands of said Hinton, Thomas Roundtree,
John Walton and Jacob Powell...

Jno. Walton
Jacob Powell

James Powell

179 2 Jan 1830--Thomas Morgan to Abram Morgan...$55...horse and cart
2 feather beds 2 spinning wheels sow and pigs chest pot skillet creep-
er 5 barrells of corn and stock of fodder...

Thos.L. Spivey
Collen(x)Morgan

Thomas(x)Morgan

179 25 Jan 1826--John Evans and wife, Mary, to John Matthews...$18
4 acres formerly property of Robert Parker, dec. and 1/6 legal share
of said Parker's estate adjoining lands of John Matthews, John D.
Pipkin, Bryant Brothers, Nancy Bond and Betsy Bullock...

Robert Cozzens
Isiah Matthews

John(x)Evans
Mary(x)Evans

180 8 Jul 1826--Thomas Collins and wife, Nancy and Robert Parker
to John Matthews...$28...8 acres formerly belonging to Robert Par-
ker, dec. and 2/6 of one legal share in division of his estate,

adjoining lands of John D. Pipkin, William Parker's heirs, Richard
Parker's heirs and Daniel Southall...

Riddick Trotman
David Costen

Thomas(x)Collins
Nancy(x)Collins
Robert(x)Parker

181 30 Jun 1826--Ezekiel Lassiter and wife, Nancy, to John Matthews
$18...4 acres, 1/6 legal share of land of Robert Parker, dec. adjoin-
ing lands of John Matthews, John D. Pipkin, Bryant Brothers, Nancy
Bond and Betsy Bullock...

Isaiah Matthews
William Polson

Ezekiel(x)Lassiter
Nancy(x)Lassiter

182 1 Jan 1827--Nathaniel F. Savage of Nansemond to William Hudgins
$200...150 acres, formerly called Merry Hill, binding on Andrew
Matthews...

R. Rawls
Mathew M. Dyes

Nathaniel F.Savage

183 4 Jun 1830--John W. Harrell to Andrew Harrell...$1.00 and to
secure to Joel B. Hurdle and Riddick Hunter for $167 note to Jos-
eph Riddick...1 horse 10 head cattle 31 head hogs double gig and
harness single jig 30 barrells of corn 48 cider barrells 4 hogshead
hand mill apple mill trough platform 2 pairs cartwheels household
and kitchen furniture...

Jas.P.Small
Noah Hurdle

John W.Harrell
Andrew R.Harrell
Riddick Hunter
Joel B.Hurdle

184 22 Jun 1830--Whitmill Hill to Edward R. Hunter...$1.00 and to
secure to Joseph Gordon note of $56.50...37½ acre tract he purchased
from Isaac R. Hunter adjoining lands of Dr. Richard H. Parker, Joseph Speight, said Hill and others...

Rich'd H. Parker

Whitmill Hill
Jos. Gordon
E.R. Hunter

185 18 Aug 1830--Riddick Hunter to Robert Hill...$1.00 and to make
safe to Joseph Gordon for becoming security to Thomas Twine, guardian to heirs of Isaac Hunter, dec. in note of $427.39...land where-
on he lives...

T. Gary

Riddick Hunter

185 11 May 1830--Nathan Ward to Joseph Gordon...$1.00 and to se-
cure a note of $500 to Thomas Twine...50 acres whereon he lives
beginning at crossroads and along road to Jethro H. Riddicks...

M. Norfleet

Nathan Ward
Jos. Gordon

186 14 May 1830--Joseph Gordon, trustee for Etheldred Mathews, to
David Benton...1 mare 1 still ox cart and wheels yoke of stears
and yoke 5 head cattle 11 head sheep 20 hogs 3 feather beds 6 win-
sor chairs 8 flags bottom walnut table 2 pine chests 1 bofat 1 desk
and books 3 iron pots 1 oven 1 griddle and gridiron 1 looking glass
2 sets knives and forks Negro man, Charles, 1 horse and wheels
brass candle stick 2 tubs 2 pails 2 prong tongs and shovel apple
mill...

Henry Pugh & William Arnold

Jos. Gordon

187 17 Feb 1830--E.R. Hunter to John Walton...$260...Negro boy,
Joe, 14 years old...

                                             E.R.Hunter
Jos. Riddick

25 Jun 1830--Henry Pugh to James Lassiter...$300...605 acres be-
ginning in center of 3 oaks near head of Reedy Branch to Daniel
Duke's corner gum with his line to run of Bennetts Creek to Lassiters corner NW to gum in Deep Branch...

                                             Henry Pugh
Jno. Gatling
L.L.Bond

188 23 Feb 1830--Henry Costen to James Lassiter...$200...200 acres
S side of Bennetts Creek beginning at a cypress on main run of creek
to mouth of Iron Mine Branch, up branch to a gum to corner of Costen':
land to main road leading to courthouse to John Gatling's line SW to
Deep Gut and adjoining Frederick Jones...land formerly held by James
Hodges, sold to Willis Woodley, then to Andrew Woodley and by Andrew
to James Costen, who willed it to his son, Henry...

                                             Henry Costen
Elisha Hays
Thomas W. Hays

189 5 May 1829--John V. Sumner, sheriff, to Jethro H. Riddick...
$100.25...100 acres belonging to James Roundtree adjoining lands
of Jesse Hobbs, Whitmill Stallings and others. Sold by deputy,
Moses B. Harrell, to comply with execution of 6 writs in favor of
Richard H. Parker, Andrew Baker, Leonard Martin (Jacob Richardson,
real plantiff), Cynthia Brinkley, Peter B. Minton and John Brinkley.

                                             Jno.V.Sumner
E.R. Hunter
R.H. Parker

190 30 Jul 1830--William Parker to James Morgan...$1.00 and to se-
cure $100 note to David Benton...Negro woman Tamer and children
Mary Ned and Milley...

                                             William Parker
John Wiggens

190 13 Feb 1830--David Lewis to Jeremiah Dixon...$625...3 Negro
girls Patty, Mila and Aggy...

                                             David Lewis
H. Gilliam

191 2 Jun 1828--David Outlaw to Henry Gilliam...$300...700 acres
beginning at Seth Spivey's line on Warrick Swamp or Welch's Mill
Pond down swamp to Catherine Creek to Old Town Landing up creek to
Mill Pond formerly belonging to George Outlaw now Jacob Parkers tp
said Spivey line to main road leading to Old Town...

                                             David Outlaw
Ro. Riddick
Lassiter Riddick

192 21 Dec 1829--Chowan: William D. Rascoe, sheriff, to Henry Gilliam...$460.50...Negro slave, Spencer, property of James R. Creecy
sold by a court writ at instance of Josiah Collins for two sums:

$7,400.07 and $191.78...

Wm.D.Rascoe

Edwin Bond
Aug. Moore

192 8 Feb 1830--Joshua Dail and wife, Milly, of Perquimans to
William Bond...$40...10 acres 25 poles, part of land inherited from
father, Richard Bond, on S side of Bennetts Creek, and a tract of
low ground in Watery Swamp...

Joshua Dail

John Hare
J. Walton

Milly(x)Dail

193 20 Nov 1828--Daniel Franklin and wife, Mary, of Nansemond to
Jethro, James A. and Thomas W. Ballard, their sons and sons-in-law,
160 acres on S side of Catherine Creek adjoining lands of John Mitchell, Peter B. Minton and others...

Daniel Franklin

Jno. Brinkley
Benjamin Franklin

Mary Franklin

194 17 May 1830--James R. Riddick, sheriff, to Henry Gilliam and
Nathan Riddick...$216.45...137 acres belonging to Abel Rogerson, ad-
joining lands of James Baker, Jasper Trotman and others...

J.R. Riddick

Jno.C.Gordon
Wm. Cowper

195 31 Oct 1828--John V. Sumner to Jesse Hudgins...$1415...187 acres
belonging to John P. Hudgins adjoining lands of Rissop Rawls, and heirs
of Josiah, William and Joe Hudgens...sold by court writ...

Jno.V.Sumner

J.R.Riddick

Sheriff

196 May Ct. 1830--John V. Sumner, sheriff, to John Riddick...$596
300 acres belonging to Stephen Rowe and sold by court order to pay
debts to John Beeman, R. Gatling, H. Eure, Wm.W. Cowper and Goodman
and Walton...adjoins lands of John B. Baker, Nancy Gatling and Wm.
L. Boothe...

Job R. Hall
Micajah Riddick

Jno.V.Sumner

198 27 Apr 1830--James R. Riddick, sheriff, to Reuben Hinton...$50
50 acres belonging to James Washington adjoining lands of Nathaniel
Jones, Noah Hinton and others...sold by court writ at instance of
David Parker...

J.R.Riddick

H. Gilliam
J. Riddick

198 3 Aug 1829--James R. Riddick, sheriff, to Aaron Pearce...$102
150 acres belonging to William Hudgins, adjoining lands of David
Riddick and others...sold by court writs of William Walton, Hamlen
L. Epps and Mary Goodman for $1051 debts...

Thomas Twine

James R.Riddick

199 3 Aug 1829--Mathew M. Dyes to Abram W. Parker...$375...Negro
man, Ben...

Matthew M.Dyes

Jno.Beeman
Condition of above sale whereas said Dyes was security for William
Hudgins to notes to Louisa Pugh, Abram W. Parker and Demsey Parker...

200 11 Mar 1830--Nathaniel Jones to James Trevathan...$36.75...12¼
acres of land on Flat Branch beginning at ditch a dividing line between said Trevathan and Noah Hinton running to Mary Washingtons,
formerly Mary Feltons, corner W and N to lands of Charles Smith,dec.

Nathaniel(x)Jones

David Parker
J. Walton

200 11 Mar 1830--James Trevathan to John Walton...$1.00 and to se-
cure a $50 bond to John Roberts...two parcels of land on Flat Branch,
one where he now resides adjoining lands of said Walton, Noah Hinton,
Nathaniel Jones and heirs of Charles Smith, dec. and containing 10 3/4
acres. The other tract of 12¼ acres adjoins lands of Noah Hinton, Mary
Washington (formerly Felton), Nathaniel Jones and Smith heirs...

James(x)Trevathan

David Parker
John Jones

John Walton
John Roberts

201 15 Jan 1828--Hardy Eason, Jr. to William Eason...$60...14 acres,
his lot No. 6 in division of estate of his father, Frederick Eason...

Hardy(x)Eason

Jos. Gordon
Jas. Granbury

201 22 Aug 1829--Wesley Knight to John Beeman...$300...Negro man,
Isaac...

Wesley Knight

Wm.L. Boothe

202 20 Feb 1830--Abram Parker to Miles Parker...$55...20 acres join-
ing lands of Miles Parker, John Benton and Edward Knight, dec.

Abram(x)Parker

James Perry
Humphrey(x)Parker

203 8 Jan 1830--John Speight to Nathaniel Eure...$149.25...90½ acres
on W side of road leading to Manney's Ferry beginning at a corner of
said Eure's NW to a white oak a corner of Joshua Lang's S to a lightwood stake to Kings Tract SE to road and along road...

Peter Eure
Abrm.W.Parker

John Speight

204 24 Mar 1830--Jethro H. Riddick to Leah Roundtree...$111...Walis
Tract formerly belonging to James Roundtree, dec. purchased by said
Riddick at sheriff's sale...beginning at run of Catherine Creek Swamp
at a gum a corner tree of Jesse Hobbs along his line SW to Whitmill
Stallings NW to forked cypress and back to swamp...

Jet.H.Riddick

Daniel S. Ward
Quinton H. Trotman

204 14 May 1830--James Costen to Isaac R. Hunter...$45...5 acres
beginning at post oak a corner tree between them on W side of main
road leading from Suffolk to Edenton W to line between Costen and
Edward R. Hunter...

                                                    James Costen
Thomas R. Costen
Jacob E. Hunter

205 5 Mar 1830--Isaac R. Hunter to Henry Riddick...$50...8 acres
beginning at black gum a corner tree betweem them on E side of road
leading from Suffolk to Edenton W to fork and then N...

                                                    I.R. Hunter
Thomas Costen
Henry Briggs

205 28 Jun 1829--John Eure Sr. to John Sparkman...$15...3 acres
beginning at red oak on Joseph Smith's line running S through Eure's
field to a gum in main run of Cypress Swamp to Fortis Land Road N
on Sparkman's line...

                                                    John(x)Eure Sr.
Abrm.W.Parker
Bray Parker

206 10 May 1830--Henry Gilliam to John Mathews...$90...2 tracts, 22
acres and ½ acres, beginning at main road in Henry Skinner's corner
SW to Gilliams own line near stables...

                                                    H. Gilliam
Law.L.Daughtry
Seth Mathews

207 1 Apr 1830--Nancy Bond to John Mathews...$65...12 acres bounded by
lands of Bryant Brothers and others and formerly belonging to Robert
Parker, dec...

                                                    Ann Bond
Briant Brothers
Jos. J. Barnes

107 29 Mar 1830--Thursy Parker to John Matthews...$18...4 acres
bounded on E,W and N by lands of said Matthews and on S by land of
Nancy Bond...

                                                    Thursy(x)Parker
Jos.J.Barnes
Jn.A.Riddick

208 23 Sep 1829--William A. Halsey of Virginia to Job Blanchard...
$65...12 acres binding on land of Henry Bond, separated by a branch
from the land of Polly Brisco, and binding on main road opposite the
meeting house...

                                                    Wm.A.Halsey
H. Gilliam
James Boothe

209 17 Apr 1830--Job Blanchard to Samuel Brown...$65...12 acres
binding on lands of Henry Bond and separated by a branch from Mary
Brisco and Mary Hudgins and on main road opposite Methodist Meeting
House...

                                                    Job Blanchard
Peter Boss
Wm. Holland

209 2 Nov 1830--James R. Riddick, sheriff, to Kicheon Norfleet and
Pryor Savage...$1.41 3/4...254 acres of land belonging to heirs of
Thomas Riddick. Sold to comply with court orders at instance of
Lassiter Riddick, David E. Sumners, Job R. Hall, James Boothe and
James R. Riddick and writs in favor of John Gatling, Micajah Riddick
and Henry G. Williams amounting to $2930.75. Land is resided on by
Joseph Riddick, son of said Thomas, and which Thomas purchased of
Jethro, David E., Thomas and Edward Sumners, Lewis M. Jiggetts; and
adjoining lands of John Figg, James Figg, Mills R. Fields, John R.
Norfleet and others...

J.R. Riddick

Jno.R.Norfleet

210 1 Nov 1830--Jacob Eason Sr. to son, Jacob Jr...gift of Negroes
Jack, Betsy and children, Soloman and Martha...

Jacob(x)Eason

William Hurdle

210 1 Nov 1830--Mary Harrell of Gates to daughter, Fanny Eason...
Negro man Robbin and all her stock of cattle, 1 bed and furniture
and household and kitcheon furniture...

Mary(x)Harrell

John C. Gordon
Wm.W.Stedman

211 28 Feb 1831--Hertford County: Samuel Eure to Augustus Moore...
$5...137 acres and to secure debt of $180.12 to firm of John N.
White and L. Weston...land beginning at Sarum Creek at Deep Branch
along road to Nathan Cullens line to a maple a corner of said Eures,
Abram W. Parker and said Cullens lines to a gum then along Coles
Creek to Tinson Eure's...

Samuel Eure
Aug. Moore
Cyprian R.Cross

212 18 Aug 1830--Simmonds Roundtree and wife, Elizabeth, to Thomas
Saunders...$60...24 acres N side of Bennetts Creek beginning at a
pine near branch at edge of creek swamp in dividing line of land
which Nancy Bond and Mary Craper drew in division of Robert Parker,
dec. land, NE to corner pine then SE...to Saunders line and down his
line to Mary Brothers(formerly Mary Parker's line). The land being
Lot No. 8 that Jane Brown drew in division of land of Robert Parker,
dec...

Simonds Roundtree
Elizabeth(x)Roundtree

Mills Roberts
J. Riddick

213 24 Jun 1830--William G. Daughtry to Mike Reed...$50...31 hundred
and sixteenth of an acre...at Gates courthouse beginning at stone on
Honey Pot Street opposite N corner of Jesse Brown's house NW to Isaac
Pipkin's on said street and NE to T. Saunders to corner between said
Daughtry and Reed...

W.G. Daughtry

L.G. Darden
Thos.L.Johnson

214 17 Aug 1830--James R. Riddick, sheriff, to Joseph Gordon...
20 cents per acre for 250 acres belonging to Moses B. Harrell and

sold by court writ in favor of Holliday Walton. Land adjoins lands
of Joseph Riddick, William Harrell and others and is part of land
whereon Moses Briggs formerly resided and was given by him in his
will to Abraham Harrell and wife and after their death to Moses B.
Harrell...

J.R.Riddick

Wm. Cowper

214 21 Aug 1817--Kedar Ellis to Reuben Ellis...200 pds...Negroes,
Hannah and Amey and her child, Lydia, and to raise and educate, Marm-
aduke and Elizabeth Ellis, children of Mary Ellis, now wife of said
Kedar. Negroes were left to Mary by her husband, John Ellis, dec...

Kedar(x)Ellis

Jos. Gordon
Reuben Ellis

215 13 Aug 1830--John G. Liles and wife, Ann, to Andrew Harrell...
$125...Lot No. 4, which was allotted to said, Ann, in division of
estate of her father, William Brothers, dec. and containing 27 1/3
acres...

John G. Liles
Ann Liles

Riddick Hunter
John W. Harrell

216 22 Mar 1830--Lemuel Elliott and wife, Rachael, to Jesse Mathias
$80...33 1/3 acres adjoining Calvin Brinkley, Kedar Ellis and Jesse
Mathias and is on main road leading to Suffolk. It was drawn by said
Rachael in division of lands formerly belonging to Elisha Brinkley,
dec...

Lemuel Elliott

William Blanchard
Rachael(x)Elliott
B. Blanchard

217 10 Aug 1830--Edward R. Hunter to Richard H. Parker...$1000...
3 tracts of land. First, 144 acres begins at red oak a corner of
said Hunters in Hills line to edge of creek; second, 57 acres, begins at persimmon tree in Sumners line SE to Eason's corner to
edge of swamp and third, 3 acres, on main road running SW to Rice's
line to line of Riddick heirs...

E.R. Hunter

Bn.B.Blanchard
I.R.Hunter

218 10 Jun 1830--Isaac R. Hunter to Whitmill Hill...$150...37½ acres
which he purchased of James Speight adjoining lands of Dr. Richard
H. Parker, Joseph Speight, said Hill and others...

I.R. Hunter

E.R.Hunter
Rich.H.Parker

218 15 Feb 1830--James R. Riddick, sheriff, to Henry Willey...$200
332 acres belonging to David E. Sumners of Hertford, sold by a writ
of Fieri Facias from county court of Hertford at instance of Edward
Shaw Nov term 1820. Land begins at a pine a new corner made in Nisum

Cuffs line SW to John Ellin and said Willeys to new road, a corner
of Mills R. Fields to a post oak a corner of Mary Parker's NW to
Vanns House to corner of Levin Cuff and said Willeys binding on
George Kittrell...

J.R. Riddick

Open Court

219 18 Aug 1829--James R. Riddick, sheriff, to William G. Daughtry
$550...lot belonging to John F. Hayes at Gates courthouse by lands
of Thomas Saunders, John Matthews and Isaac Pipkins. Sold by a
court writ brought by Hamilin L. Epps for $250 and interest against
Joel Hudgins and John F. Hays...

J.R. Riddick

Jno. Riddick
Law.L.Daughtry

220 25 Jan 1830--Abel Rogerson to Nathan Riddick...$175...27 acres
adjoining lands of Elisha Trotman, heirs of Riddick Trotman, dec.,
Leah Roundtree and others...it being land which Penelopy White, wife
of Benbury White, drew in division of real estate of her father, Riddick Trotman, dec...

Abel Rogerson

Jet.H.Riddick
Jesse Rogerson

221 21 Dec 1829--Riddick Gatling to John Lee...$50.62...22½ acres
beginning at a pine a corner of said Gatling's line on E side of
ditch S to Abraham Parker's line along his line SW to sweet gum a
corner in John Sparkman's line and NE...

Riddick Gatling

William Gatling
Joseph Gatling

222 22 Mar 1830--Benjamin Blanchard Sr. to son, Absolom...$300...50
acres beginning at pine in William Blanchard's opposite meeting house
to a pine on edge of Beaverdam Swamp on swamp to fork of branch at
Pearce's fence...plantation whereon he lives...

B. Blanchard

William Blanchard
Mary(x)Brothers

222 16 Aug 1830--Thomas Eason to Joseph Speight...$125...50 acres
beginning at pine a part of marsh on Bennetts Creek E to a post oak
in Whitmill Hill's line and along his line W...land he purchased
from Moses and David Speight...

Thomas(x)Eason

Wm.W.Stedman
Jesse Mathias

223 5 Dec 1826--Riddick Hunter to Andrew Harrell...$575...two tracts
of land...the first, 100 acres, begins at public road at Mary Hintons
line to Greens line to Robert Riddicks line and down road. Second
tract of 44 acres he purchased of Joseph Gordon on N side of Horsepool Swamp adjoining lands of Abraham Harrell, which he purchased of

John Moran; David Harrell and lands of Abraham Harrell, heirs of
Henry Harrell, dec. and binding on Mill Pond at high water mark...
Riddick Hunter
Jos. Gordon
Mills Roberts

223 1 Jun 1829--Nathan Riddick to son-in-law, Elisha Hunter...gift
of 49 acres, known as the Hurdle land, beginning at James Brinkley's
line S along Henry King's line to Trotmans line to run of Catherine
Creek Swamp up run to Milton Eason's line N to James Brinkley's
line and W...
Nathan Riddick
Jet.H.Riddick
John Voight

224 15 Nov 1828--Isaac Green to son, Riddick, gift of plantation,
whereon he lives, 43 acres beginning at long-strawed pine at end
of ditch to a gum in Cypress Swamp down swamp to Judith Harrell's
line to a pecosin pine in Lewis Green's line...
Isaac(x)Green
Wm.L.Boothe
Margaret(x)Green

225 14 Nov 1828--Isaac Green to son, Lewis, gift of 25 acres in
Sand Banks adjoining Long Pond beginning at a corner pine at upper
end to a red oak in Mills Sparkman's corner to Martha Taylors line
to a long-strawed pine near end of ditch to a persimmon tree...
Isaac(x)Green
Wm.L.Boothe
Margaret(x)Green

225 31 Jul 1830--John Figg to James Brown...$40...20 acres beginn-
ing at a pine in James Figg's line N to John Lewis line E and then
S along William Cleaves line to a pine a corner of Cleaves and W...
John Figg
William Hudgins
Sam'l R. Morgan

226 13 Aug 1830--Andrew Harrell to John G. Liles...$225... 100
acres N side of Horsepool Swamp beginning at high water mark adjoining lands of Joseph Gordon, John Alpin and others...surveyed
by John Bogue...
Andrew Harrell
Riddick Hunter
Jno.W.Harrell

226 20 May 1830--John Brinkley to Jesse Mathias and Riddick Jones
$800...Negro man Jim, woman Fanny and girls Rachael and Malvina...
Jno. Brinkley
Jas.A.Ballard
Benjamin Brinkley

227 9 Nov 1829--Solloman Riddick to Abraham Riddick...$400...175
beginning at Old Orapeak Swamp Col. Josiah Riddick's line down
swamp to Etheldred Mathews line and along his line to post oak in
edge of road to James Jones line to James Morgan to William Minors.
Solloman Riddick
John Mathews
Margaret(x)Norfleet

227 23 Feb 1830--David Benton to Seth Benton...$150...64 acres
whereon Moses Jones now lives beginning at red oak William Barrs,
dec. line to a gum in Flat Branch NE to said David's...

David(x)Benton

James Morgan
Ethel'd Matthews

228 8 Jun 1830--Moses B. Harrell to Andrew Harrell...$1.00 and as
trustee for $1100 in debts...all land,corn and bacon,double gigg,
quantity of leather at Josiah Briggs and his rights in cattle in
possession of William Eason. All rights in land containing 17 acres
belonging to William Barnes, dec. and purchased for taxes; 20 acres
belonging to Jethro Brinkley, 13 acres of James Powell's,38 acres of
Peter Boss' sell to pay debts to the following: John W. Harrell and
William Harrell for support of his family during his imprisonment and
to John V. Sumner, Riddick Hunter, Benjamin Ballard, Benjamin Brinkley, William Brinkley, Demsey Hall, Whit Hill, Samuel Jackson, Noah
Speight, Joseph Hurdle, Robert Alpin and Theophulis White...

M.B. Harrell

Jeremiah Rogerson
H. Gilliam

A.R. Harrell
Riddick Hunter

230 23 Oct 1830--Jethro Willey to Henry Gilliam...$1.00 and pay-
ment of a $2000 bond to John Willey...Negroes Eanos, Melia, Aggy
and Isaac and 5 head cattle and 1 sorrell mare...   Jethro Willey
Henry Gilliam

W.G. Daughtry

John Willey

231 25 Oct 1830--Andrew B. Harrell to John Liles...$1.00 and to
secure to Willis W. Harrell $205.87½ which he has paid to Mary
Goodman...two tracts of land: one which was allotted to his wife,
Julia, in division of estate of William Brothers, dec. and is Lot
No. 1 and contains 44 acres. The second tract of 37 acres was allotted to Ann Brothers in same division...also 2 horses, 5 head hogs
and all household and kitchen furniture...

Andrew R. Harrell

Seth Harrell
I.S. Harrell

Willis W. Harrell
John G. Liles

232 22 Mar 1830--James A. Ballard to Abraham Riddick...$500...two
tracts of land. First, 100 acres of high land he heired from his
father's estate adjoining lands of John C. Gordon, Tilly W. Carr,
Richard H. Ballard and others and the second tract is ½ of lot of
20 acres in White Oak Spring Marsh adjoining lands of heirs of William Fontain, dec...

James A. Ballard

Jos. Gordon
Demsy Vann

232 30 Jan 1830--Stuard Bond to George Costen...$5...his share of
timber on Bennetts Creek, which fell to him by death of his father,
Richard Bond...

Stuard Bond

James Lassiter

233 39 Jan 1830--Ailsey Bond to George Costen...$5...her share of
timber, which fell to her by death of father, Richard Bond...

Jos.W.Riddick

Ailsey(x)Bond

233 5 Apr 1831--Robert Williams to Henry Deel...sold by court order
1 black mare, horse and cart and wheels, formerly property of James
Fore of Pasquotank...$21.87½...
                                                    Robert Williams

234 22 Jan 1830--Benjamin Sumner to Kicheon Norfleet...$640...60 acres
which Jethro Sumner obtained by patent 1 Sep 1800 beginning at red oak
in line formerly Thomas Smiths on Bennetts Creek Swamp to gum in line
formerly George Williams and SW and another tract of 300 acres conveyed by Pasco Turner to Elizabeth Sumners by deed 18 Jan 1796,known by
name Hilly Swamp. A third tract which was conveyed by Jethro and Elizabeth Sumners to him by deed 27 Feb 1826 and adjoining lands of John
R. Norfleet and heirs of Jonathan Williams, dec...
                                                    Benjamin Sumner
Jno.R.Norfleet
Tinson Eure

235 21 Dec 1829--William Eason to Pleasant Speight...$10...12½ acres
adjoining Charles and Seneth Eason and is Lot No. 5 in division of
father's pocosin land...   William Eason
Jas.P.Small
John W. Harrell

235 2 Oct 1830--James R. Riddick, sheriff, to George Costen...$1.00
and $68.46 to comply with court writs against lands of Humphrey Hud-
gins, dec. in hands of William and Joel Hudgens. Land whereon he
died and gave to William Hudgins and joins lands of Levi Beeman,
heirs of Micajah Riddick, dec. and others...
                                                    J.R.Riddick
William Cowper
Wills Cowper

236 14 Jan 1830--Division of Negroes of John Ellis, dec. made by
Joseph Hanneford, in right of his wife, Ellizabeth, and Marmaduke
Ellis: Lydia $250, Ishmel $65, Sally $80, Katy (life right), and
Drusilla to Mary; Amy and child, Caroline $250, Wright $180 and
Hannah to said Marmaduke.
                                                    Jos.W. Hannaford
M. Norfleet   Marmaduke Ellis
John R. Donnell, circuit judge

237 7 Apr 1831--John W. Harrell to Joseph Gordon...$150...249 acres,
all that tract of land formerly belonging to Moses Briggs, dec. adjoining lands of Joseph Riddick, William Harrell and others...which
said John W. purchased from his brother, Moses B. Harrell 14 Dec 1829.
Jesse Brown   John W. Harrell
J.R. Riddick

238 16 Feb 1830--H.Gilliam to Jesse J. Cox...$175...½ acre lot at
Gates courthouse, bounded on N by main road, S by lot of Jesse Brown
and on E by said Gilliam...   H. Gilliam
Nathan Riddick
Jethro Willey

239 14 Aug 1830--Richard H. Parker and wife, Emaline, to Edward R.
Hunter...$1400...land which she inherited from her father, Micajah
Riddick, dec. beginning at black gum near main road leading from
Middle Swamp to fork of road E to Wild Cat Springs to Bennetts
Creek SW to road bounded on N by James Murdaugh, E by Thomas E.
Riddick, S by John Beeman and George Costen and W by road...

                                                Rich.H.Parker

Ben.B.Ballard   Emeline Parker
I.R.Hunter

240 20 Sep 1830--Willis W. Harrell to Andrew R. Harrell...$300...
1 acre, his part of land formerly belonging to his father, and whereon he lives...

                                      Willis W. Harrell

James P. Small
I.L. Harrell

240 18 Dec 1814--Mills Lewis to John Brady...$32.50...6½ acres,
a small piece of woodland, beginning at a pine corner of Brady's
own line and John Warren's land N to corner of John Vann's and on
Brady line...   Mills Lewis

William Goodman

241 25 May 1829--John Brady to Kindred Parker...$160...50 acres
beginning at paw paw gum in main run of Petersons Swamp in Isaac
Pipkin's line and corner of said Kindred's thence along his own
line to a water oak a corner of William Sears and along his line
to a water oak standing near Brady's field, a line of marked trees
to a black gum near edge of swamp and to main run of swamp...

                                    John Brady

William H.Goodman
John Saunders

241 23 Sep 1830--Moses D.H. Jones to John Benton...$58.13...2 carts
and wheels and corn crop on land of Richard H. Ballard...

                                  Moses D.H.Jones

Jos. Gordon
James Morgan

241 23 Sep 1830--Lewis, Ira and C. Carter to Jacob Odom...Negro
boy, Isaac for $53...

                                  Lewis(x)Carter
                                  Ira(x)Carter

Jno.Beeman   C. Carter

242 8 Apr 1829--William Hays to Richard Hays...$90...40 acres be-
ginning at ash standing in Deep Bottom running to John Waltons to
Timothy Hayes and to Hollow Bridge to main road leading from courthouse to Hunters Mill and down road to corner and to John Hays line...

                                  William Hays

Rich'd Cross
Charles Williams

243 7 Dec 1829--James R. Riddick, sheriff, to Timothy Walton...
$202.51...30 acres belonging to Timothy Freeman, dec., now in hands
of his heirs. Sold by court writ issued by Whitmill Stallings and
Andrew Baker. Land is well-known as Trotman Bagley tract, adjoining
lands of said Walton, heirs of Timothy Walton Sr. dec, Jeremiah White
and others...
                                                    J.R. Riddick
Open Court

244 3 Nov 1830--James R. Riddick, sheriff, to Timothy Walton...$10
75 acres belonging to Thomas L. Spivey, whereon he lives adjoining
land belonging to Riddick Trotman, bounded on the W by John White
and James Eure, S by Daniel Eure, E by Noah Roundtree and W by Isaac
Hyatt. Sold by court writ issued against said Spivey by Whitmill
Stallings for $426.77...
                                                    J.R. Riddick
Open Court

245 1 Mar 1831--Etheldred Mathews to John Powell Jr., infant son of
Thomas Powell, dec...$25...25 acres bounded on N by Old Ferry Road,
which divides it from Charles Powell; on S by land belonging to heirs
of John Outlaw; on E by land of John Taylor and Jacob Parker and on
W by Catherine Creek...
                                                    Ethel'd Mathews
John Mitchell
Wm.W.Stedman

246 16 Nov 1830--Lassiter Riddick, guardian to Elizabeth, Sarah C.,
Mary and Julia Riddick, infant heirs of Thomas Riddick, dec., to
James Boothe...$288.99...275 acres adjoining lands of Lewis Walters,
Nisum Cuff, Mills R. Fields and land belonging to heirs of Henry
Lassiter...
                                                    Lassiter Riddick
Jno. R. Gilliam
Ro. Riddick

247 20 Sep 1830--Andrew R. Harrell to Isaac S. Harrell...$375...
land adjoining lands of Robert Riddick, James Davis and others...
                                                    Andrew R. Harrell
Jas. P. Small
W.W. Harrell

247 30 Aug 1828--Tilley W. Carr to James Carr, James S. Seguina and
Frederick William Carr, all of Norfolk...$50...all juniper timber on
tract of pecosin land on N side of Chowan River opposite mouth of
Meherrin River known by name Woights Ferry, which he purchased of
John Waddle for 6 years...
                                                    T.W. Carr
Humphrey Parker

248 20 Aug 1830--Riddick B. Eure to Tinson Eure...$250...100 acres
beginning in branch near road to corner red oak in Jethro Eure's
line to a corner on John Beemans to a water oak a corner of Asa Harrells and John Beemans to a pawpaw gum in Coles Creek to Gum Branch.
                                                    Riddick B. Eure
Wm.L.Boothe

248 30 Jul 1829--Clement Hill to Henry B. Lassiter...$93...31 acres
on road leading to Parkers Landing beginning at a pine corner of Mrs.
Parkers land and along road to Hills Avenue...

Clement Hill

M. Roberts
John Roberts

349 14 Nov 1830--Lemuel G. Darden to John R. Norfleet...$50...Negro
boy, Harrison...

Lem'l G.Darden

T. Garey

350 2 Oct 1830--James R. Riddick, sheriff, to John Beeman...$1.00
and court costs of $68.46...160 acres belonging to Humphrey Hudgins,
dec. in hands of William and Joel Hudgins, executors, and is the
plantation whereon he lived and died. Sold by court writ.James R.Riddick

251 2 Oct 1830--James R. Riddick, sheriff, to Rissup Rawls...$1.00
and $68.46 court costs...160 acres of land belonging to Humphrey
Hudgeons, which he gave to his son, Levin, in his will; adjoining
lands of Noah Harrell, dec., heirs of Josiah Hudgins, dec and Levin
and Joel Hudgins...

J.R. Riddick

Wills Cowper Jr.
William Cowper

252 25 Oct 1830--James R. Riddick, sheriff, to Nathan Riddick...$175
150 acres of Jesse Hudgins, sold by court writ at instance of John V.
Sumner for $1013.50...adjoins lands of William Cleaves, John Figg,
Mills R. Fields and others...

J.R. Riddick

Open Court

252 20 Aug 1830--John Beeman to John R. Norfleet...$1500...150½
acres, land whereon Humphrey Hudgins formerly lived and died and
conveyed by will to his son, Joel...beginning at ditch in line of
Micajah Riddick's heirs to main road and along road to George Costens.

Jno.Beeman

Wm.L.Boothe
Wm.E.Pugh

253 25 Oct 1830--Benjamin Knight to Demsey Knight...$150...110 acres
beginning in Elm Swamp in said Demsey's line down run to Orapeak Swamp to line of John Hare's, dec. to Brinkley Henderson's line...

Benjamin Knight

I. Sumner
John Gary

254 20 May 1829--Margaret Jameson to John Brady...$160...95 acres,
which descended to her by death of her child, William E. Jameson
(minor) beginning at pawpaw tree a corner of Kindred Parker's in
Peterson Swamp along his line to water oak a corner in William Sears
line along his line to corner between said Parker and Brady...

Margaret Jameson

John Saunders
Wm.H.Goodman

255 20 Mar 1830--Henry Jones to Thomas Cornelius of Nansemond...$50
109 acres beginning at black gum in Sumerton Creek in Hare's line
SE to pine in Willis Duck's line, SW to creek and then N...

H.H.C.Jones
Timothy(x)Howell

Henry Jones

256 27 Oct 1830--Thomas Walton to Hardy Eason...$250...70 acres on
W side of main Virginia road adjoining lands of said Hardy, Nathan
Cullens and others...

Thos.L.Spivey
W. Walton

Thos. Walton

257 9 Sep 1830--Jesse Mathias to Edwin Mathias...$400...68 acres
bounded by lands of Daniel Ward, Calvin Brinkley and Cader Ellis...

James A. Ballard
James Mathias

Jesse Mathias

257 25 Oct 1830--William Speight to Wills Cowper Jr...$192...38 acres
tract formerly belonging to Pleasant Babb, dec., which he heired from
her estate and his brother, John Speight, dec., adjoining land of
Seth and Augustus Morgan and heirs of John Granbury, dec...

Jos. Gordon
Geo.G. Harvey

Wm.W.Speight

258 2 Feb 1831--Jonathan Parker of Rutherford Co., Tn. letter of
attorney to Hillory Willey to let or sell land in Notty Pine Swamp
beginning at live oak S to white oak in William Baker's line E to
a pine and N to a branch...
John R. Laughlin, clerk of
court of justice, Murfreesborough
Wm.M.Murray and William Gilliam
justices

Jonathan Parker

259 10 June 1830--William Arnold to Abraham Riddick...$83.60...63
acres beginning in state line and running S to line of heirs of
John Brothers, SW to Orapeak Swamp and up swamp to line of chopped
trees NE to state line...

Ethel'd Matthews
Lemuel L. Powell

William Arnold

259 8 Nov 1830--Jesse Matthias to Demsey Vann...$96.09...60 acres
joining Josiah Riddick and others...

Jos. Gordon
Abraham Riddick

Jesse Matthias

260 4 Nov 1830--Demsey Vann to Abraham Riddick...$190...60 acres,
whereon he lives, for which Jesse Mathias holds a mortgage...adj-
oining lands of Josiah Riddick and others...

Jesse Mathias
Jos. Gordon

Demsey Vann

260 26 Dec 1829--Frederick Hinton Jr. to Thomas Hinton...$125...29½
acres on main road leading from courthouse to Edenton beginning at
a ditch on side of road, a corner on land of Sarah Lewis, dec. running E to a tract of land that said Thomas purchased from John Walton and that Walton purchased from heirs of Robert Lassiter, dec. N
binding on said Thomas line to Docton Hays to a post oak and to main
road from courthouse to Sunsbury. It is the land wereon Thomas Hinton now lives and a part of that belonging to William Hinton, dec.
and sold to Frederick Hinton, to make a division...

                                                    Frederick Hinton
Noah Hinton

261 12 Feb 1831--Joseph J. Barnes to Louisa Cross of Hertford with
H. Gilliam as trustee: Whereas a marriage is shortly intended to be
solemnized between said parties and all real estate, personal estate, money and choses in action of said Louisa should be secured...
for $1.00 to Henry Gilliam, in trust, The Outlaw Track containing all
land in Speight's old patent running to Odom's line, formerly Dick-
insons on edge of Mirey Swamp and following Negroes: Isaac, Jail,
Penina, Rachael and children, feather bed and furniture, all agree-
able to will of Abraham Cross. Rents on property to be paid to said
Louisa at any time she may direct and if she should die first all
property to go to her legal heirs. Said Barnes will not injure, waste
or convert to his own use any property, rights, credits or choses,
which may come to his hands and said Louisa is not to be liable for
any of his debts...

                                                    Louisa R. Cross
Jno Bond   Jos. J. Barnes
Henry W. Skinner   H. Gilliam

263 28 Dec 1830--Lassiter Riddick to James R. Riddick...$1375...500
acres bounded on E by Honey Pot Swamp, S by main road and lands of
Edward Riddick heirs and lands of Job R. Hall, land whereon William
W. Riddick now lives and conveyed by deed of trust by him to said
Lassiter 17 Nov 1828...

                                                    Lassiter Riddick
Jno.D.Pipkin
Willis I. Riddick
      William W. Riddick releases his interest in above tract. Wit-
nessed by M. Roberts and John Beeman...

265 5 Jan 1831--James R. Riddick to John Roberts with John Walton
as trustee...For $1450 note due said Roberts...500 acres whereon
William W. Riddick now lives bounded on E by Honey Pot Swamp, S
by main road and land belonging to heirs of Lassiter Riddick, dec.,
N and W by land of heirs of Edward Riddick, dec. and Job R. Hall;
also Negroes Miles, William, Isabella and child, Lewis, Allis and
Rachael and 2 brandy stills...

                                                    J.R.Riddick
John Bond   John Roberts
Jas. T. Freeman   J. Walton

266 21 Oct 1830--Willoughby Manning to James Morgan...$1.00 and

to make safe to David Benton $100 note...Negro woman, Dilley,
22 years old...

Willoughby Manning

John Benton

266 21 Oct 1830--James R. Riddick to William Wright...$375...Neg-
ro man, Aly...

J.R.Riddick

Jam. C. Riddick
H. Wright

267 10 Feb 1831--Whitmill Eason of Talbot County, Ga. authorizes
his friend, Whitmill Stallings, as his attorney...

Whitmill Eason

268 2 Sep 1829--Joseph J. Barnes to Jethro Sumner...$150...100
acres undivided 2/5 part of land belonging to Benjamin Barnes, dec.,
who died intestate, and his land descended to his heirs of which
said Joseph is one and is entitled to 1/5 part and second 1/5
belonging to heirs of William S. Barnes, which he bought by court
decree, for debt due to him from estate. Land adjoins lands of
Robert Riddick, heirs of John Riddick, dec., Edward R. Hunter and
others...

Jos.J.Barnes

Open Court

268 23 Dec 1830--Mills Riddick, court clerk, to John C. Gordon...
$327...77 acres, petition filed by James P. Small, Elisha Small
and others, belonging to Andrew I. Small, and 60 acres of desert
land adjoining...

Mills Riddick

John Gatling
James R. Riddick

269 27 Dec 1830--Thomas W. Ballard to John C. Gordon...$68.83...
87½ acres, ½ of a patent of Jethro Ballard, dec. 1 Nov 1779, binding on lands at present owned by said Gordon, William W. Stedman,
Jethro Ballard, who owns other half, and Henry Lassiter, dec...

Thomas W.Ballard

T.W. Carr
Kedar Ballard

270 10 Jan 1831--William Reed to Henry Riddick...$325...Negro woman,
Lovely, and child, Edmond...

Will.Reed

Burwell Brothers
William Eley

270 1 Jan 1831--Robert Riddick to Henry Riddick...$50...20 acres
beginning at post oak, a corner tree between Robert and Henry,
running E to a sweet gum to a red oak a corner between Robert and
Edward Briggs SE to a persimmon tree on E side of Canal Ditch...

Robert Riddick

Jacob Powell
James Briggs

271 23 Feb 1831--Abraham Beeman to son-in-law, Jesse Brown...gift
of a tenement in town of Gatesville on W side of street leading to
Somerton, Va. between lots of Abraham Parker and Jesse C. Cox...

Abm. Beeman

Wm.L.Boothe

272 29 Mar 1830--John B. Harrell to Nathaniel Harrell...$225...50
acres on W side of Coles Creek beginning at white gum running down
creek to Jethro Eure's to Spring Branch and up branch...

John B. Harrell

James Smith
W.R. Moore

273 19 Nov 1830--Asa Harrell to son, Nathaniel, gift of land W side
of Coles Creek, about 2 acres, beginning at pine standing on ditch
in Spring Branch NW between two dwelling houses and running NE...

Asa Harrell

Reuben and Elisha Harrell

273 1 Jan 1831--Charney Umphlett and wife, Elizabeth; Thomas Hoggard and Nathan Smith to John Beeman...$125...31 acres beginning
at black gum in Little Cypress Swamp a corner tree of John Eure's
line thence along Penelope Carter's line to an oak, a corner tree
in Reuben Parker's line, with Parker's line to a pine a corner tree
in Abram Beeman's line to head of Hawtree Branch and down branch...
land which descended to them from Mary Smith, wife of Joseph Smith,
as her heirs at law...

Charney(x)Umphlett
Elizabeth(x)Umphlett

Wm.L.Boothe
Jesse Parker

274 15 Jun 1830--Willis Duck to Henry Jones...$50...109 acres be-
ginning at small ash on Somerton Creek SE to Thomas Cornelius line...

Willis Duck

H.H.C.Jones

275 8 Feb 1831--John B. Boyes of Madison County, Tn. and William
Boyes of Lincoln County, Tn. to Jacob Odom...$150...150 acres be-
ginning at a pine on edge of Reedy Branch, a corner of Burwell
Griffith and Abraham Cross, running Cross line to Sand Banks and
to Odom's line...

John B. Boyes
William Boyes

John L.I. Griffith
Rich. Odom

275 18 Feb 1831--David Riddick to son, Elbert, gift of 164 acres
of land he purchased of Esther Mathews and known by name of Coles
Island in Merry Hill Pocosin...

David Riddick

Seth R. Morgan
David F. Felton

276 4 Dec 1830--Hetty Crafford to Abraham Crafford...$5...bay horse,
cow and yearling, red heifer, feather bed and furniture and all
household furniture...

Hetty Crafford

Jacob Odom

276 28 Aug 1830--Humphrey Parker to David Benton...$706...four
Negroes Abram, Merida, Jacob and Sam...

Humphrey Parker

James Morgan

276 19 Feb 1831--Joseph Gordon to John Alpin...$12...6 acres, part
of a 12½ acre tract sold to Abraham Harrell beginning at post oak
in said Alpin's and Gordon's corner N to main road and E to branch
and then W...

Jos. Gordon

M. Norfleet
M. Ellis

277 28 Jul 1820--George Harrell to Thomas Wynns of Hertford...$20
100 acres beginning at a gum on main road leading from Wynns Ferry
to Norfolk near Arnolds Ridge and down pecosin to edge of swamp and
then SW...

George(x)Harrell

Isaac Speight
Jas. D. Wynns

278 23 Nov 1830--Jacob Odom to Abraham Smith...$600...300 acres be-
ginning at corner gum in Burwell Griffiths and Odoms line in Mirey
Branch to corner pine of Odoms and Abraham Cross to corner juniper
in edge of river and down pecosin...

Jacob Odom

Richard Odom
John L.I. Griffith

279 2 Dec 1830--Timothy Walton Jr. to Absolom Blanchard...$210...
mill that formerly belonged to Timothy Walton, Sr., bounded on N
by lands of Henry Bond, S by land of heirs of said Timothy Sr.,
contains 1 acre on N and 3 acres on S...

Timothy Walton

Jas.R.Billups

280 16 Aug 1830--Jesse Mathias to James Lassiter...$325...Negro
man, Abram, 28 years old...

Jesse Mathias

Henry Costen

280 25 Oct 1830--James R. Riddick, sheriff, to Jethro H. Riddick...
$5...50 acres belonging to heirs of Isaac S. Riddick, dec. adjoin-
ing lands of Abram Hurdle, Hardy Eason, Isaiah Riddick, Joseph
Riddick and others. Sold by court writs issued for the following
debts by: Nathan Riddick-$78.84, Isaac R. Hunter-$25.72, Josiah
Jones-$45.30, Henry Gilliam-$33.25, Edgar Whitehead-$22.98, Pas-
cel Jones-$13.88, Josiah S. Jones-$48.49...

J.R. Riddick

Open Court

281 19 Feb 1831--Jethro Sumner of Nansemond to David Howell...$100
½ of seine place known by name Dowery with 2 acres of land on Chowan
River...

Jethro Sumner

William Davidson
Soloman Daughtry

281 19 Feb 1831--William Davidson of Nansemond to Soloman Daughtery of Isle of Wight...$100...½ of seine place or fishery called Dowery with 2 acres land on Chowan River, which was conveyed by deed of bargain 24 Jan 1774 from John Giles to Elisha Duke and bequeathed to Jonathan Rogers by said Duke...

William Davidson

Jethro Sumner
D. Howell Sr.

282 3 Feb 1831--John Brinkley, Jesse Mathias and Riddick Jones to John Benton...$400...Negro man, Jim...

Jno.Brinkley
Jesse Mathias
Riddick Jones

Jno.Wiggens

282 21 Feb 1831--Demsey Bond to son, Elisha H., gift of land on N side of Bennetts Creek, stock, household furniture, plows, cart, mare, corn and all other property...

Demsey Bond

Henry Jocelin
Quinton(x)Roberson

283 18 Feb 1829--James Costen to his relatives: Timothy Lassiter-Negro boy, Garrison, Sally M. Lassiter-Negro girl, Lucy, Mary E. Lassiter-Negro girl, Mary...

James Costen

James Lassiter

283 17 May 1831--John V. Sumner to Henry Gilliam...$5.58 for unpaid taxes on 97 acres, part of a tract listed by Peter Boss, beginning at stake in Brown's line a corner of Benbury Walton and running NW...

Jno.V. Sumner

Whit Stallings
Abel Rogerson

284 17 May 1831--Jno. V. Sumner to Benbury Walton...$5.14 for 1829 taxes on 190 acres on main road from courthouse to Edenton between Beaverdam and Indian Swamps and beginning at a stake in Brown's line a corner of Henry Gilliams E to Pearce's line...

Jno. V. Sumner

Wm.E.Pugh
Henry R. Pugh

285 10 Jan 1831--Humphrey Parker to Joshua Jones...$225...45 acres beginning at black gum in small branch in John Barnes line across cornfield SW to a maple in Rutha Brinkley's line to Solloman Ellis line to a red oak a corner in Kedar Taylor's line...

Humphrey Parker

Demsey Knight
Eliza Parker

285 10 Nov 1830--Exum Lewis to Susannah Piland...$175...58 acres beginning at a holly, a corner tree of Demsey Eure's, Demsey Sparkman and James Goodwin thence to a white oak, a corner tree of John

Lewis(orphan of John Lewis, dec.) and Nathan Cullens line thence
to Winton Road...

                                        Exum Lewis
Wm.W.Cowper
Wm.L.Boothe

286 20 Mar 1829--William W. Cowper to Susannah Piland...$450...80
acres beginning at gum in main road along line of John B. Bakers to
run of swamp to William Sears line and along his line to main road...

                                        Wm.W.Cowper

Jno. Riddick
Peter Piland

286 14 Feb 1831--William Hofler to Abram Morgan...$150...50 acres
in fork of two swamps--Beaverdam and Indian; a line between said
land and John B. Walton's, down swamp to mouth of Schoolhouse Branch to Beaverdam and to edge of high land...

                                        William Hofler

Thomas S. Spivey
James T. Freeman

287 27 Dec 1830--Thomas W. Ballard to Jason Franklin...$400...
200 acres beginning at post oak on main road leading from Suffolk
to Edenton W to stob drove up at back line of heirs of John Brothers,
dec. N to state line and E to a lightwood stump and S...

                                        Thomas W. Ballard

Jno. O. Hunter
William Arnold

288 6 Mar 1830--Abraham, Soloman and Josiah Riddick to Josiah Riddick
of Nansemond...$1000...mill seat and 75 acres called Powells Mill,
binding on N by lands of Josiah Riddick, S by William Miner, E by
Kedar Ballard and David Brinkley and W by James Morgan and Humphrey
Parker, which more fully appears in will of John Powell Sr. and
given to John Powell Jr...
Jacob D. Bagley   Abraham Riddick
James Riddick   Soloman Riddick

288 23 Feb 1831--Nathan Riddick to John Lewis...$80...40 acres
bounded on S by lands of said Lewis, W by James R. Riddick and N
by Mills R. Fields...

                                        Nathan Riddick
J.R.Riddick
John Figg

289 23 Feb 1831--Nathan Riddick to John Figg...$93.50...46 3/4
acres beginning at black jack oak SW to small pine near Figg's
fence, to Honey Pot Swamp and up swamp to gum below James R. Riddick's dwelling and SE...

                                        Nathan Riddick
J.R. Riddick
Jno. Lewis

289 26 Jan 1828--Abraham Riddick and now wife, Elizabeth, of Nan-
semond to Mike Reed...$40...20 acres beginning at pine a corner of
Miles Benton and heirs of David Parker, dec. SE to pine stump and
NW to a lying down pine in William Parker's corner...
Ethel'd Matthews   Abraham Riddick
Jacob D. Bagley   Elizabeth(x)Riddick

290 10 Mar 1813--Kindred Carter to Alexander Carter...$7.34...his
interest in tract of land on Cypress Swamp, which descended to him
by death of his late sister, Annis... (Note: This date was written
1813 but it might should be 1830)...
                                                    Kindred Carter
Bray Parker
Stephen Lee

291 27 Nov 1830--Benjamin Hays to William G. Daughtry...$45...34
acres beginning at small cypress, a corner of No. 8 in division of
land formerly belonging to Robert Parker, dec., now owned by Thomas
Saunders, SW across and island along creek to run of branch which
empties into creek, down run of creek to a black gum at old land
and NW...
                                                    Benjamin(x)Hays
Robert Cozzens
Law. L. Daughtry

291 22 Feb 1831--Henry Gilliam to Elijah Harrell...$192...52 acres
conveyed by deed of trust from Soloman Roundtree for debts owing
Daughtry and Webb, adjoining Benjamin Hays and others...it being
two tracts purchased from Thomas Riddick...

Lassiter Riddick   H. Gilliam
Jno.R.Gilliam

292 27 Nov 1830--Isaac Pipkin to Elijah Harrell...$300...100 acres
on N side of Bennetts Creek beginning at road where run of swamp
crosses, to Moses Davis line to Deep Branch along Benjamin Hays line
to pine at clay hill and down road...it being the lot of land which
fell to John Parker, son of Robert Parker, dec. and bounds described
in division of land of said Robert...
                                                    Isaac Pipkin
Robert Cozzens
Pryor Savage

293 21 Feb 1831--Reuben Hinton Sr. to Noah Hinton...$21...5 acres
on E side of Flat Branch beginning at run near a white oak in said
Reuben's line and binding on said Noah's and down run...
                                                    Reuben Hinton
J. Walton
Kedar Hinton

293 23 Apr 1831--Joseph Small to Isaac R. Harrell...$1.00...100
acres and to make safe to Joseph Gordon and Holloday Walton notes
given to Jethro Ballard for said tract of land, which adjoins John
Powell...
                                                    Joseph(x)Small
James(x)Alpin   Jos. Gordon
Dan'l(x)Gwin   Holloday Walton

294 29 Dec 1830--Jethro Ballard of Nansemond to Joseph Small...$250
100 acres binding on lands of Richard A. Ballard and John C. Gordon.
Joshua Jones   J. Ballard
Holloday Walton

58

295 24 Aug 1830--Ann N. Harvey to William W. Cowper...$408.33...
122½ acres beginning at planted rock on E side of road leading to
courthouse SW to Wiggens Bridge up Gauf Swamp NE and then SE to
J.D. Pipkin's ditch...
Ann N. Harvey
Jno.D.Pipkin
William B. Harvey

295 29 May 1830--Charles and Ira Carter to William Sears...$25...
Negro girl, Mary, 3 years old...
Charles Carter
Abrm.W.Parker
Ira Carter

296 16 Apr 1831--Charles and Ira Carter to William Sears...$40...
black mare, cart and wheels, cow and yearling...
Charles Carter
Jesse Parker

296 24 Mar 1831--David Lewis to Thomas Saunders...$275...Negro
woman, Patty, 18 years old...
David(x)Lewis
Jo. Riddick
J.R.Riddick

297 26 Jan 1831--Benjamin B. Ballard to William W. Stedman...$84
1 gray and 1 sorrell horse, 1 mule, 7 sheep, 1 looking glass, 2
waiters, 2 tables, candlestick and irons, Negro Aesop...
Edward Briggs
Bn.B.Ballard

297 4 Mar 1830--Holloday Walton to son-in-law, William W. Stedman,
gift of 174 acres of land, whereon said Walton lives, which he
bought of Noah B. Hinton, a part of which said Stedman now holds,
adjoining lands of heirs of John Granbury, dec., John Gwin and
others...said Walton to hold life estate...
Holloday Walton
James Lassiter
Joseph Gordon

298 11 Apr 1831--D. Parker to Isaac L. Harrell...$22.80...his
interest of Moses B. Harrell and wife, Nancy, in Negro, Nancy
was entitled to by will of Samuel Harrell, dec. and sold under
an execution by Henry Pugh 21 Mar 1831...
D. Parker
Burwell Brothers

299 9 Oct 1831--Chowan County: Augustus Moore to Henry Gilliam,
trustee of James R. Creecy, dec.....$200.10...Soffa, side board,
pair of looking glasses, carpet, 18 chairs, 50 fenders, andirons,
shovel and tongs, silver, settee, dinnerware, vegetable dish, 10
plates, 2 tumblers, cup, china, knives, forks and tray, waiters,
candlestick, snuffers and tray...
H.W. Skinner
Aug. Moore

299 9 Apr 1831--William E. Pugh, Henry Pugh and Henry Gilliam
bound to Munford Stokes, governor of North Carolina for 2000
pounds...appoint Wm.E. Pugh, clerk of court...Wm.E. Pugh, Henry Pugh
Jeptha Fowlkes
H. Gilliam

300 10 May 1830--Leah Roundtree to Whitmill Stallings...$8.00...
8 acres, the Wales Tract, formerly belonging to James Roundtree,
dec. beginning at a red oak on side of the tract, SE to a pine on
S side of tract and NW to a post oak and dogwood...

Leah(x)Roundtree

Dan'l L. Ward
Quinton H. Trotman

300 May Ct. 1831--Robert Riddick by deed of trust of Abel Rogerson
to Joseph Riddick...$350...Negro woman Charlott, Boy Henry, Girl,
Mary...

Ro. Riddick

H. Gilliam

301 16 Feb 1830--Division of lands of William Beasley and wife, Mary,
and Henry Jones, tenants in common and fee: Survey No. 1--William
Beasley...40 acres 3 roods beginning at red oak NW to white oak in
Miles Parker's line NW to a cypress and along run of Cypress Swamp.
No. 2--Henry Jones...40 acres 3 roods beginning at cypress at corner
of No. 1 in swamp to a pine, a corner in Miles Parker's line. No. 1
to pay No. 2 $18...

Miles Howell
John Speight
Jason Saunders
Willis Cross

302 9 Feb 1831--Division of land of Robert Saunders, dec., containing 981 acres and on which Jason Saunders now lives. Valued
at $1200. Lot No. 1--Jason Saunders, the house tract beginning at
sweet gum near road leading to Manneys Ferry SE to run of Deep
Cypress Swamp up run to water oak, a new corner between No. 1 and
No. 2, along dividing line SW to a persimmon tree at edge of swamp
in Exum Jenkins line, where he made a purchase of 2 acres for a
mill seat, NW to a pine corner of Miles Parkers in a small pond
then to a pine corner of Isaac Jenkins. Lot No. 2--Drew M. Saunders
186 acres beginning at water oak on edge of Deep Cypress up swamp
to a dead oak a corner of Elizabeth Lee and James Williams in little
pocosin to post oak near orchard. No. 3--Robert Saunders...345 acres
beginning at post near orchard to a white oak a corner of James Williams in little pocosin SW to a water oak to path that leads to Winton Ferry then to Joseph Freeman and Speight's line. No. 4--Gilbert
Saunders...270 acres beginning at persimmon tree in cornfield, a
new corner made in Lots. 1,3 and 4 SW to a path leading to Winton
Ferry NW to hickory and dogwood to near edge of Cypress Swamp. No.
4 to receive from No. 1 $10 and from No. 3 $45. Each to pay $5.71¼
in expenses...

Jason Saunders
Robert Saunders
Drew M. Saunders
Gilbert Saunders

R. Gatling
Nath'l Eure
John Speight

304 Feb Ct 1826--Division of estate of Thomas Parker, dec. legatees
in Brinkley vs. Parker: No. 1--William Brinkley, by right of his
wife...100 acres beginning at red oak near Jesse S. Hare's and

Jacob P. Jones corner SW to small gum lying down SW to David Bentons
N to a stake a corner of Abram Riddicks SE to a small elm Humphrey
Parker's corner and then to an oak near said Parkers avenue and SW.
No. 2--Jethro Brinkley by right of his wife...74 acres beginning at
a small gum a corner of David Bentons and William Brinkleys SW to a
red oak... No. 3--Margaret Ann Ballard...74 acres beginning at pine
corner on Jethro Brinkleys and David Bentons SW and then N to Abram
Riddicks and then SE to corner of Riddicks and Brinkleys. No. 4--
Jordon Parker...74 acres beginning at sweet gum in Margaret Ann
Ballards corner SW to David Bentons N to Riddicks. No. 5--Alfred
Ballard by right of his wife...74 acres beginning at pine a corner
of David Bentons and Jordon Parkers NW to Riddicks and S. No. 6--
Alfred Parker...74 acres beginning at pine corner on David Bentons
and Alfred Ballards and NW and then S. No. 7--Kedar Ballard by right
of his wife...74 acres beginning at a stake a corner of Bentons and
Alfred Parkers NW to David Bentons to John Bentons and Abram Riddicks.
No. 8--Mary Odom...74 acres beginning at a small pine a corner on
David Bentons and Kedar Ballard NW to red oak to corner of Josiah
Ellis and John Arnolds then NE to a corner in John Bentons and Kedar
Ballards. Alfred Ballard to pay Jethro Brinkley $185, Alfred Parker
to pay Margaret Ann Ballard $166.50 and Jordan Parker $18.50 and
Kedar Ballard to pay Jordan Parker $74.

                                          James Morgan
                                          Jacob P. Jones
                                         ·Humphrey Parker

305 15 Nov 1826--Division of extate of James Knight, dec. left
to his sons, John and Benjamin, and land whereon he lived. Survey
of 122 acres to Benjamin...along main road from swamp S to Benton's
line. Survey of 170 acres on W side of road to heirs of John Knight,
dec. as follows: No. 1--Savage children...30 acres adjoining swamp.
No. 2--Benjamin Knight...28 acres. No. 3--Elisha Ellis and wife...
28 acres. No. 4--Demsey Knight...28 acres. No. 5--James Knight...28
acres and No. 6--Mary Fields...28 acres...

                                          Wm.W.Stedman
                                          James Morgan
                                          Ethel'd Matthews
                                          C.E. Sumner

306--Nov Ct. 1822--Division of estate of Isaac Walters, dec. in
Walters vs Walters: 435 acres divided as follows: No. 1--Charles
Walters...203 acres beginning at small dogwood corner on William
Babbs running NW to a black gum in branch to a small white oak on
Elisha Parker's, dec. and Robert Wilson's along Wilson's line SE
to Riddicks pocosin, a corner on said Wilson, William Doughtie and
Winburn Jenkins, dec. SW to a corner on Jenkins and John Babbs to
a branch a corner on John and William Babbs and NW. No. 2--Simon
Walters...232 acres beginning at black gum in branch, a corner on
Hardy D. Parker's and William Babbs running said branch to corner
on Elisha Parkers, dec and Charles Walters to small dogwood in
William Babbs corner SW to a sassafras, corner of William Babb,
Daniel Williams and William Matthews and binding on Matthews to

Blake Bakers to a post oak, a corner on Thomas Gomer, dec. and
George Smith, thence running Smith's line NE to a pine, a corner
of Smith and Babb. No. 1 to pay No. 2 $130.50...

H. Willey
George Kittrell
Hardy D. Parker

Daniel Parker, county surveyor

308 26 Oct 1829--Division cf estate of Jesse Brown: Survey No.
1--William Brown...57 acres beginning at a pine a corner of William Blanchard's in Benjamin Brown's line NE to a large pine to a
line of Henry Waltons heirs SE to a maple a corner of Robert Parker and wife and Sarah Brown's in said Benjamin's line and SW. No.
2--Robert Parker and wife, Louisa...91 acres beginning at a sweet
gum a corner of Timothy Walton's on side of old road SE to a maple
a corner of William Brown and Sarah Brown. No. 3--Sarah Brown...91
acres beginning at a maple a corner of William Browns and said Parkers NE to a small persimmon to a dead pine a corner of Walton Freemans on side of old road SW to willow oak...

Walton Freeman
William Walton
Timothy Walton

Alternates: Benjamin Blanchard
         Henry Bond

309 1 Nov 1825--Division of estate of Moses H. Small: Survey No.
1--James P. Small...119 acres beginning at cypress stump in Loos-
ing Swamp corner on John C. Gordon and heirs of Thomas Ballard, dec.
running SE to white oak stump then NE to edge of desert to Campbells
line. No. 2--Andrew I. Small...95 acres beginning at pine corner on
said Gordons SE to desert to Campbells and to high land. No. 3--Tho-
mas A. Small...101 acres beginning in land in front of house at Andrew's corner SE to a gum stump to corner on Gordons NE to desert
to Campbells line and high land. No. 4--Sophia A. Small...114 acres
beginning at Edenton Road in front of William W. Stedmans and Richard Smalls corner SE and then SW to a red oak a corner of Benjamin
Jones and Robert Riddicks to a piece of undivided land called The
Ridge one mile from W side of the desert, containing 50 acres. No.
5--Eliza T. Small...88 acres beginning in front of Stedmans house
to corner of Ballards and Elisha Small and SW. No 6--Christian
Small...88 acres beginning at small pine at road corner of said
Eliza's SE and then SW to Jones and Riddicks corner and NW along
road...Each survey valued at $250...

R.H. Ballard
William(x)Miller
Robert Riddick

Joseph Gordon
Holloday Walton, alternates

310 Aug Ct 1828--Division of estate of Milly Bond, formerly Milly
Barnes: Lot No. 1--Etheldred Cross in right of wife, Cherry, formerly Cherry Barnes...44 acres beginning at small pine bush a new
corner made between 1 and 3 and in Capt.Richard Odom's line SE to
a pine on edge of old field SE in a kind of hedgerow to a corner of
Capt. Odoms and NE to new dividing line. No. 2--Benjamin Barnes...
44 acres beginning at a pine a new corner between 1 and 2 to a corner of Capt. Odom's and Jacob Odom NE to out boundary line to a

lightwood post to corner of Benjamin Barnes and heirs of Etheldred
B. Gatling. No. 3--heirs of Etheldred B. Gatling...44 acres beginn-
ing at lightwood post NE to an ash a corner of Elisha Bond and Capt.
Odom...

Alternates:
Abraham Beeman
Abraham Cross

Willis Cross
Levi Eure
Jacob Odom

314 6 June 1827--Division of estate of Henry Harrell: Survey No.
1--William Harrell...60 acres 2 roods beginning at a sweet gum in
Horsepool Swamp in Joseph Gordon's line S to a corner of said William and Creecy's line NW to a corner of Jesse Y. Harrells and down
run of swamp. This includes 6/10 of the survey, his 1/10 and the
following that he purchased 1/10 each from: Noah Harrell, James
Harrell, John G. Wilson in right of wife, Mary, Moses B. Harrell
in right of wife Nancy. He is to pay $7.50 each to Isaac and Jesse
Harrell. Survey No. 2--Andrew and Willis Harrell (by consent)...
20 acres 1 rood or 2/10 of the survey beginning at black gum in
corner of Joseph Gordons SW to a persimmon tree in corner of 3 and
1 to Creecy's line to willow oak in Ridge Branch, a corner of Abram
Harrell and down branch. No. 3--Isaac Harrell...10 acres 1 rood
beginning at corner of said Andrew and Willis in Creecy's line SW
to a pine stump a corner of Jesse's SE to pine at head of Horsepool
Swamp. No. 4--Jesse Y. Harrell...11 acres beginning at persimmon
tree a corner of Isaac and William's SW to head of Horsepool Swamp
and NE...

Benbury Walton, surveyor
Isaac S. Riddick, alternate

Jos. Gordon
Wm.W.Stedman
J. Riddick
John Alpin

31
315 Aug Ct. 1827--Division of land of William and Joseph Crafford,
dec. 658 acres including the following four tracts: first adjoining
lands of George Harrell, Asa Odom, Abram Cross and others; second
adjoining lands of Peter Boss, Asa Odom and others; third adjoins
lands of Peter Boss and wife, Oday, Richard Odom and others and the
fourth is known by name Half Moon Fishery on Chowan River with pecosin land adjoining and lying on Buckhorn Creek and Arnold's Ridge.
The whole tract begins at Black Hole on Wynns Ferry Road running SE
and N to beach to run of Cypress Swamp. Division to the tenants in
common as follows: No. 1--John Crawford...175 acres; No. 2--Rach-
ael Landing...161 acres; No. 3--Elizabeth Howell and No. 4--Oda
Boss...161 acres. John Crawford and Elizabeth Howell are listed
as infants...No. 1 to pay No. 3 $53.25 and No. 4 $2.00 and No. 2 to
pay No. 4 $53.25.

Alternate:
Rodon Odom

Abm. Beeman
Richard Odom
John Beeman
Levi Eure

315 Nov Ct. 1829--Division of land of John Brother, dec. between
heirs: No. 1--William Arnold...60 acres and No. 2--Soloman Riddick...43 acres. The whole tract of 106 acres is bounded on N by

Virginia line, which separates it from Abraham Riddick, on S and E by
John Brothers, dec and on S and W by swamp...   T.W. Carr
Alternates: James Morgan
Humphrey Parker   Jesse Mathias
Demsey Knight
John F. Hays, surveyor.

316 12 Aug 1829--Division of land of Josiah Hudgins, dec. Survey
No. 1--Soloman Roundtree in right of wife, Amelia...54 acres be-
ginning at stake a corner of No. 2 SW to sweet gum. No. 2--William
I. Hudgins...60½ acres beginning at stake NE to ditch and to beach.
No. 3--Louisa Hudgins...46½ acres beginning at red oak running to
road NE to Rissop Rawls SE to Noah Harrells corner. No. 1 to pay
No. 3 $47.50, No. 2 to pay No. 3 $55.67½ and No. 2 to pay No. 1
$23.20...   Pryor Savage
                                                   Simmonds Roundtree
Alternates: John Matthews
Richard Smith
Noah Harrell

318 6 May 1819--Division of estate of Mills Williams: Survey No. 1--
Nancy Williams...15 acres beginning at small sweet gum a corner of
William Hudgens on side of road thence along road to a corner of
Allens line. No. 2--Elizabeth Williams...20 acres beginning at white
oak a corner of No. 1 SW and then N to Allens line. No. 3--Martha
Williams...25 acres beginning at maple a corner of Elizabeth's SW
to a blackjack. No. 4--Sophia Williams...25 acres beginning at a
blackjack at a corner of Martha's SW to Allen's line. No. 5--Jordon
Williams...28 acres beginning at post oak a corner of Sophia's in
Allen's line to head of small branch. No. 8--Robert Williams...25
acres beginning at black gum in Hilly Swamp and NE down swamp to
Allen's path. No.6--Benjamin Williams...34 acres beginning at a
corner of Jordon's in small branch to a sassafras SE to branch. No.
7--Lovina Williams...35 acres beginning at black gum in Hilly Swamp
NE to Allen's path and SW to swamp. No. 9--Allen Williams...30 acres
beginning at water oak in Hilly Swamp to Maple Branch and SW. Jordon
to pay Elizabeth $28 and Nancy $4. Benjamin to pay Martha $5 and
Elizabeth $1. Lovina to pay Martha, Sophia, Robert and Allen $4
each...   Richard Smith
Alternates: Joshua Allen
John Matthews   Jesse Hudgins
Jonathan Williams

319 4 Jul 1831--James R. Riddick, sheriff, to James Lassiter...
$200...100 acres belonging to John Lewis, dec. adjoining lands of
James Booth and heirs of Demsey Jones. Sold by court order to recover $300 owed to said Lassiter...   J.R. Riddick

D. Parker
Lassiter Riddick

320 5 Oct 1831--John Pruden to Willis F. Riddick...$1.00 and to
secure debts for which James Pruden is security...11½ acres known

as the Jethro Riddick Place containing 150 acres and belonging to
his father, James Pruden Sr. and where said John now lives and
bounded by lands of David Riddick, John Matthews, Wilie Riddick
and others. Also Negro man Jim sorrel mare and horse colt 12 head
cattle 20 of hogs 15 stands of bees 4 feather beds and furniture
2 walnut tables half dozen Windsor chairs 1 bofat stone crockery
glassware pots teakettle Dutch oven all household and kitchen
furniture 2 carts and wheels and farm utensils...to secure notes
of $95,$34 and $385.50 to Wilie Riddick...

John Pruden
Elbert H. Riddick   Willis F. Riddick
Thomas Smith   James Pruden

320 19 Oct 1831--Perquimans County: William Reed and wife, Elizabeth to Miles Elliott Jr...$2000...900 acres adjoining lands of
Isaac Hunter, dec., heirs of Frederick Eason and others and is the
manor plantation of Benjamin Gordon, dec., which was divided between
said Elizabeth and her sister, Mary Hunter, who conveyed her half to
Elizabeth 1 Feb 1825...

W. Reed
Jesse Wilson   Elizabeth Reed
James Martin, ct. judge

322 4 Mar 1831--Myles Elliott to William Reed...$2000...The above
tract of land...½ of which was conveyed by Mary Hunter to her sister, Elizabeth Lassiter 1 Feb 1825.

Myles Elliot
Open Ct.

322 4 Mar 1831--Nancy Riddick to Isaac Pipkin Sr...$200...Two tracts
of land...the first of 67½ acres called the Elvey Lewis tract, which
James Gatling Esq. purchased from Elvey Lewis, begins where Judey
Branch empties into Mills Swamp along branch to said Gatlings line
binding on Christian Lewis line to Wet Slash and to new line made
by James Riddick and Pryor Savage to Mills Swamp; 2nd tract of 20
acres was purchased by said Gatling from Elizabeth Lewis, begins at
sweet gum in Mills Swamp to Isaac Pipkins line and down swamp...
Jno Gatling   Nancy(x)Riddick
John Riddick

323 7 May 1831--Benbury Walton to Henry Riddick...$400...two Negroes
Ben, about 12 and Mary, 13...
Benbury Walton
Sarah Freeman

324 12 Aug 1830--Walton Freeman to Peter B. Minton...$500...griss
and saw mill on 2 acres land and mill seat known by name Walton Mill
and formerly property of James Walton and more recently of said Free-
man's father, Timothy Freeman,which he purchased at his father's sale
bounded by land of Waltons and Nathan Cullens on the N, said Minton,
Frederick Rooks and others on the S...
Walton Freeman
Whitmill Stallings
John Willey
Jetho H. Riddick

324 16 May 1831--Shadrack Felton and wife, Susannah, to Penelope
Felton...$21.50...10 3/4 acres beginning at post oak in Dempsey
Sparkman's line to white oak, corner tree of said Shadrack...
Dempsey Sparkman   Shadrack(x)Felton
Wm.L.Boothe   Susannah(x)Felton

325 1 May 1830--Joseph Hurdle and wife, Candis, to Thomas Roundtree
$100...100 acres beginning at maple in John Walton's line in Reedy
Branch W and binding on William Hintons line to Mirey Branch...
William King   Joseph Hurdle
Abel Rogerson   Candis(x)Hurdle

326 18 May 1831--John Riddick and wife, Margaret, to John Willey
$190...67 acres that they drew in division of land of Mills Lewis,
dec. begins at sweet gum corner of Mrs. Wolfreys SW to road leading
from courthouse to Isaac Pipkins to small red oak standing in Kindred Parker's line SW and S on Parkers line and W to William Sears
and N to said Willeys to a white oak corner of Mrs. Hurdles...
Wm. G. Daughtry   John Riddick
Jno. Lewis   Margaret Riddick

327 10 May 1831--Jeremiah White and wife, Elizabeth, to William
Blanchard...$285...75 acres beginning at pine on edge of Beaverdam
Swamp SE to black gum corner of Benjamin Brown NE to corner of Will-
iam Brown's fence to Timothy Waltons and crook of Beaverdam Swamp...
B. Walton   Jeremiah(x)White
T. Gary   Elizabeth(x)White

328 14 May 1831--Burwell Griffith and wife, Loviney, to Josiah Mc-
Coy of Norfolk...$1000...all timber on tract known as Holley Island
Pocosin for 10 years...bounded by James Williams, Jesse Vann, James
Brady, Jacob Odom, said Griffith and William Goodman...
George W. Copeland   Burrell Griffith
Jacob Odom   Loviney(x)Griffith

329 11 Jan 1830--J.R. Riddick, sheriff, to Lassiter Riddick...$37.41
Negro man Willis, formerly property of Thomas Riddick Sr...
Mills Riddick   J.R. Riddick

329 16 Aug 1830--John D. Pipkin to Henry W. Skinner...$225...18
acres on main road from Bennetts Creek Branch to Suffolk adjoining
lands of Abraham Parker, Henry Gilliam and John Brown and beginning at corner of Methodist Episcopal Church in Gilliams corner...
W.G. Daughtry   Jno.D.Pipkin
Law.L. Daughtry

329 10 Dec 1830--Henry Gilliam to Henry W. Skinner...$25...$\frac{1}{2}$ acre
beginning at Jesse Coxes corner on Honey Pot Street SW to post on
Parkers line to corner of John Matthews...   H. Gilliam
Jephtha Fowlkes

330 21 Feb 1831--William Williams of Hertford to Jacob Odom...$30
__tract beginning at corner white oak of Burrell Griffiths in Reedy
Branch to Griffith and Boyces corner to Odoms line...
Richard Odom   Wm.(x)Williams
Barsheba(x)Jones

331 25 Nov 1830--James R. Riddick, sheriff, to James Boothe...
$181.50...3/7 of tract known as Middle Swamp Plantation and belong
ing to heirs of Thomas Riddick, dec...sold by court writ at instance
of John Gatling, Micajah Riddick, Henry G. Williams, Willis I. Riddick, Lassiter Riddick, Job R. Hall, David E. Sumners and said Boothe
for $2861.38 in debts...adjoins Lewis Walters, John Ellin, Nisum Cuff
and George Kittrell...   J.R. Riddick
Willis I. Riddick
Jno. Bond

332 7 Jan 1831--Jasper Trotman to Jethro H. Riddick...$200...Negro
girl 12 years old...
Jasper Trotman
Joseph Riddick
P.B. Minton

333 12 May 1831--Daniel S. Ward to his son, Nathan O. Ward...gift
of 56 acres that he purchased of James Baker and formerly belong-
ing to Henry Walton, dec., where he now lives adjoining lands of
Whitmill Stallings, Elisha Hunter, Seth Trotman heirs and others...
Nathan Ward   Daniel S. Ward
Joel B. Hurdle

333 12 June 1828--William Eure to Thomas Eure...½ of 12½ acres binding on John Beeman, Shadrack Felton and Jethro Eure...to be taken off
hog pen end...
Abrm.W.Parker   Wm.(x)Eure
James Williams

334 26 Mar 1831--Robert and Drew M. Saunders to Willis Cross...$50
125 acres on Sand Banks Mill Pond and river pecosin; being part of
undivided land that Jesse Saunders Sr. gave to his son, Robert Sr.
in will and that he purchased of John Copeland on E side of Chowan
River binding on Goodman land on E, Mill Pond run and Hare's line on
N to river then running James and Benjamin Saunders line and S..
Nath'l Eure   Robert Saunders
Jason Saunders   Drew M.Saunders

334 8 Nov 1830--Seth Piland to Arodi Draper...$200...Lot No. 1 of
undivided land of James Piland, dec. 56 acres beginning at pine near
new road a new corner of Seth and Elisha Piland's lots SE to ditch
in front of Mills Pilands house SE to Pryor Savage and said Mills
line to new corner of heirs of James Piland SE to John Worrells...
Robert Cozzens   Seth Piland
James Booth

335 28 Mar 1831--Robert Saunders to James Williams of Hertford...
$250...345 acres beginning at pine in Williams line to Jason Saun-
ders to a dogwood in Ann Speight's line to Freeman's line...
Rich'd Odom   Robert Saunders
Jason Saunders

336 26 Oct 1830--John B. Walton to Nathan Nixon...$200...150 acres
bounded by Catherine Creek Swamp and known by name Rawls Place...
W. Walton   John B. Walton
Reuben(x)Nixon

336 20 Jul 1830--James Baker to Abel Rogerson...$100...50 acres in
Juniper Swamp between Catherine Creek and Bennetts Creek beginning
at foot of old canal road through Juniper to Catherine Creek near
islands of Jacob Parker's line N to Turkey Pen Ridge...
Abraham Twine   James Baker
William Hobbs

337 26 Feb 1831--Charles Williams to Thomas Wright Hays...$150...
30 acres beginning at white oak in Holly Tree Branch in Benjamin
Hays line to a pine a corner on Abner Pearces to road that leads
from courthouse to Hunters Mill and to Hollow Bridge across road...
Timothy Hays   Charles Williams
Richard Hays

338 23 Jan 1830--John Ellin to Blake Baker...$20...6 acres beginn-
ing in Ellins line to water oak and S...
Nath'l Doughtie   John(x)Ellin
R. Matthews

338 21 Feb 1831--David Umphlet to Charney Umphlet...$88...30 acres
beginning at red oak, a corner in Riddick Gatling and Demsey Sparkman's line running W to Susan Beemans to Dempsey Eure's and E...
John Eure   David(x)Umphlet
Britten(x)Smith

339 2 Dec 1830--Seth Teabout to George Harrell...$50...20 acres be-
ginning at Mills Eure's line SE along pecosin and N to Long Branch...
Abrm.W.Parker   Seth Teabout
James Williams

339 23 Jul 1831--John D. Pipkin to Joseph B. Skinner...$1566...500
acres...as guardian of orphans of John Little, dec...tract of land
where he lives adjoining lands of Dr. John B. Baker, Mrs. Ann N. Harvey and the same tract conveyed to said Pipkin by Benjamin Wynns and
wife. Also, Negroes Granville, Ben and Tamer and her children Nelson
and Hagar...
Aug. Moore   John D. Pipkin

340 17 Aug 1831--John D. Pipkin to Henry Gilliam...$600...bond for
500 acres on which he lives made to John Roberts. Same land as described above and Negroes Ginny and Ester...
Jno.R.Gilliam   John D. Pipkin

341 17 Nov 1830--Lassiter Riddick to James R. Riddick...$19.25 two
tracts of 50 acres and 1 acre sold as guardian for Elizabeth C.,
Mary and Julia Riddick, infant heirs of Thomas Riddick, dec. and
4/7 part of land adjoining Mills R. Fields, Lovice Pugh and lands
belonging to heirs of Mills Williams known as Hilly Swamp...
Jas.C.Riddick   Lassiter Riddick
H. Gilliam

343 20 Nov 1830--James R. Riddick, sheriff, to Kicheon Norfleet...
$301...400 acres belonging to Thomas Riddick in hands of his heirs,
Joseph Riddick, John Riddick and Nancy Gatling(wife of William) ad-
joining lands of John Gatling, Benjamin Hays, Kicheon Norfleet and
others. Sold by court order for debts at instance of Micajah Riddick,
Henry G. Williams, Willis I. Riddick, Job R. Hall, David E. Sumners,
Lassiter Riddick and James Boothe...
H. Gilliam   J.R. Riddick
Lassiter Riddick

344 1 Aug 1831--John V. Sumner, sheriff, to Timothy Walton...$1.00
31 acres in Watery Swamp beginning at a pine a corner of James Costen and Seney Lassiter in edge of swamp NE and then S...
J. Walton   Jno.V.Sumner
James Boothe

344 20 Feb 1831--Jethro Ballard to John C. Gordon...$44.25...88½,
½ of 177 acres patented by Jethro Ballard, dec. 1 Nov 1779 binding
on lands now owned by said Gordon, Wm.W. Stedman, Lassiter Riddick
and others...
M.N. Ellis, D. Parker   J. Ballard
and Jno.R.Norfleet

345 30 May 1831--James R. Riddick, sheriff, to John Roberts...
$1.00 and to comply with court writ brought by said Roberts aga-
inst Mills Riddick, John Gatling, John V. Sumner and Jethro Sumner
for $2769.68...tract of land whereon John V. Sumners resides ad-
joining Richard H. Parker and land of heirs of the late John Riddick.
J.R. Riddick
Jesse Wiggens
John Gatling

346 19 May 1831--John Gatling to Jethro Sumner...$1600...land on
N side of Bennetts Creek, which was divised by James Barnes, dec.
to son, Joseph J. Barnes, and by him sold to Daniel Riddick and
sold by him to Charles E. Sumner, who sold to John Gatling...ad-
joins land of heirs of late John Riddick...
Jno. Gatling
Wm. Eley
Ben. Sumner

347 15 Aug 1831--Jethro Sumner to Jesse Mathias...$75...33 1/3
acres bounded by Kedar Ellis, heirs of John Tooley and heirs of
Elisha Brinkley...is tract sold by court order to make division of
land of heirs of Arthur Brinkley and bought by Jethro Brinkley and
afterward sold at an execution in favor of John C. Gordon, executor
of Thomas Parker, dec. and bought by Etheldred Mathews who sold to
Jethro Sumner...
J. Sumner
Open Court

348 7 Jun 1831--Daniel S. Ward to Abner Eason...$375...Negro, Rose,
21; Moriah, 20 mos. and Henry, 6 mos...
Daniel S.Ward
Jet.H.Riddick
Joel B. Hurdle

348 6 Mar 1827--William Pearce Sr. to Kedar Riddick...$250...94
acres W side of Great Dismal Swamp, which he bought of Arthur Pearce
beginning at Isaac Pearce's line W to Frederick Jones to John Nixon's
line and is the part of division made to Jacob Pearce's heirs and
another tract of 6¼ acres adjoining...
Wm.(x)Pearce
Jos. Gordon
Joseph Hurdle

349 15 Aug 1831--Exum Lewis to John Lewis...$55...1 work ox, cart
and wheels, 2 heifers, 7 chairs, 2 chests, 2 tables, pot, parcel of
old barrels, 3 geese, 12 chickens, 1 cupboard and furniture...it being
property purchased at sale of Soloman Green Jr. by virtue of court
execution at instance of John Freeman...
Exum Lewis
Wm.L.Boothe

349 15 Aug 1831--John Beeman to William L. Boothe...$320...Negro
man, Isaac, 32...
Jno. Beeman
Law. L. Daughtry

349 26 Aug 1829--John Barnes to Jethro Sumner...$100...50 acres,
1/5 part of land belonging to Benjamin Barnes, who died intestate,
and which descended to him as an heir...adjoining lands of Robert
Riddick, heirs of John Riddick and Edward R. Hunter...
John Barnes
Jno. Gary
Thomas Gary

350 7 Mar 1831--John W. Carter of Elberton in Elbert Co., Ga., by

Wiley Thompson, his attorney, to Mills Riddick of Suffolk...$500
900 acres in Dismal Swamp granted to William Watkins and by him
willed to his daughter, Sally, from whom the said John W. as sole
heir of said Sally and John Carter, dec., her husband, derived
title by descent. Tract begins at James Jones corner in Capt.
Cowper's line W to Col. Riddick's line E and S to county line...
Francis D. Charlton, Elliott Whitehead   John W. Carter
and William Sumner, state of Virginia   by Wiley Thompson
William Sumner and John L. Denson,
justices for Nansemond certified

351 22 Jun 1831--Isiah, Nathan and Joseph Riddick, Mabel Hill,
Jesse Rogerson and wife, Hannah, Langley Billups and wife, Esther,
to Mills Riddick of Nansemond...$600...1098 acres formerly belong-
ing to Gen. Joseph Riddick, dec. The first of 1000 acres was patented 27 Oct 1784 and begins in Abraham Hurdle's line, a part of
same patent, to Solloman Eason's and N; second tract of land was
patented 17 Oct 1784 and begins at NE corner of said Eason and
runs to lines of Joseph and Isiah Riddick and N...
Joseph Gordon   Isiah Riddick   Jesse Rogerson
William Harrell   Nathan Riddick Hannah Rogerson
Jno. W. Parker   Isaac Riddick   Esther Billups
Abraham Morgan   Mable Hill   Langley Billups

353 26 May 1831--Abraham Hurdle to Mills Riddick of Nansemond...
$80...160 acres of desert land beginning at stake on hill and E...
Jos. Gordon   Abraham Hurdle
Marmaduke N. Ellis

353 11 Jul 1831--Moses Wilkins to Barnes Goodman...$150...50 acres
adjoining Col. Jethro Sumner and William Benton...
Jno.T. Gary   Moses(x)Wilkins
Thos.S.Gary

354 20 May 1825--John T. Benton, Joseph Gordon, Richard H. Ballard
and John Hofler to James T. Freeman...$350...148½ acres on W side of
Juniper Branch in Indian Neck beginning at black gum running S to
Thomas Freeman's line to Clement Hills to Nancy Outlaw, dec. to
James Ward and Thomas Trotman, dec. and back to Juniper...
Jas. Granbury   R.H. Ballard   Jno.T.Benton
Wm.W.Stedman   Jno. Hofler   Jos. Gordon
Josiah Briggs

355 2 Aug 1831--Henry Willey and wife, Penina, to Elisha H. Bond...
$303...245 acres beginning at a black gum corner of Eff Lewis runn-
to William H. Goodman's line to Richard Odoms, to Dempsey Eure and
said Bond...a tract Penina drew from her father's estate...
Jethro Willey   Henry Willey
Elizabeth Brown   Peninah Willey

256 3 Feb 1830--John Ellin to Malachiah Cuff...$40...10 acres be-
ginning at red oak in Nisum Cuff's line NE to white oak and SE to
John William's line...
R. Matthews   John(x)Ellin
Jno.H.Haslett

257 28 Feb 1831--Garrett Hofler, trustee, for Elisha Robertson to
Reuben Lassiter...$80...127 acres adjoining lands of John Morris,
Lovina Parker, Henry B. Lassiter and John Roberts...
I. Walton   G. Hofler
Robert Williams

357 2 Sep 1829--Richard Cross to Charles Williams...$250...45 acres
beginning at black oak in William Kittrell's,dec. line to Benjamin
Hays to large swamp near Bennett's Creek...
Timothy Hays   Rich'd Cross
Richard Hays

358 24 May 1831--Benjamin Blanchard Sr. to Thomas Twine...$160...
71 acres beginning at stake a corner of William Blanchards opposite
Henry Bond's house to Pearce's line at corner of Great Marsh to wat-
er oak corner of Benjamin Browns in Benbury Walton's line to road...
Kicheon(x)Howell   B. Blanchard
John(x)King

359 7 Jun 1831--Rissop Rawls to Eli Worrell...$300...37 acres be-
ginning on main road a corner on John R. Norfleet and Worrells NE
to Noah Harrell and SE...   R. Rawls
Elisha Hays
George(x)Polson

359 10 Jun 1831--Joseph J. Lawrence of Nansemond, attorney in fact
for George W. Lawrence of Jasper County, Ga., to Henry Jones...$900
676 acres conveyed by deed to said George by Jethro Sumner 5 Feb 1828
beginning in Cypress Swamp, a corner of William Davidsons and up
branch NE to Elijah Hares and SE to heirs of Lewis Eure, dec. and
Speights...   Joseph J.Lawrence
H.D.E.Jones
James(x)Sumner

360 10 May 1831--William Blanchard to Miles Brown...$142...32 acres
beginning at white oak a corner of said Browns in Beaverdam Swamp
running NE to Timothy Waltons and SW...
                                             William Blanchard
A. Blanchard
James Blanchard

361 22 Feb 1831--Milly, Asa, Seth, Mills, Isaac, heirs of Elisha
and heirs of James Piland to Reuben Piland...$209.05...Negro slave,
Elijah...   Milly(x)Piland Asa Piland
                                           Seth Piland   Jesse Piland
Thomas Hoggard   Mills Piland   Isaac Piland
                                           Mills for Elisha's heirs
                                           Jesse for James' heirs
361 22 Feb 1831--J.R. Riddick to John W.
Parker...$136.92...Negro man Sam, property of Samuel R. Morgan, sold
by execution at instance of Benbury Walton...
                                             J.R. Riddick
Thomas Riddick

361 17 Jan 1831--Thomas Speight to Henry Speight...$150...57 acres
adjoining lands of Joshua Allen, Richard Smith and Robert Smith...
Richard Smith   Thomas Speight
W. Hudgins

361 23 Jan 1831--William Reed to James Lassiter...$500...Negro man
Arthur, 52; John 8 and Mariah 11 and 1 still...
Jordan Parker   William Reed

362 4 Oct 1831--Thomas Walton to James Harrell of Suffolk...$30
5 acres N side of Catherine Creek, part of tract recently purchased
from Milly Walton and bounded by main road from Edenton to Suffolk...
Wills Cowper Jr.   Thos. Walton
Jno. Bond
Andrew Baker

363 31 May 1831--Jethro Sumner to David Benton...$2100...250 acres
on Bennetts Creek devised by late James Barnes to son, Joseph J.,
whereon John V. Sumner now resides, adjoining land of heirs of John
Riddick, Augustus and Seth R. Morgan and others and 4 undivided 5's
of land which James Barnes devised to son, Benjamin, and which descended from Benjamin to his heirs: John, William S., Joseph J. Barnes,
Elizabeth Sumner, wife of John V. Sumner...300 acres...
Jesse Wiggens   Jethro Sumner
John T. Gary

364 6 Dec 1830--Miles and Jesse Benton and Elizabeth Jones to Luke
Green $8.00...4 acres that Bentons mother and father sold to said
Green and which they sold a life right to Jacob Gordon, in Mills
Swamp and known by name Baylis Swamp, joining heirs of William Bro-
thers, dec...   Miles(x)Benton
Jos. Gordon   Elizabeth(x)Jones
Nath'l Doughtie   Jesse(x)Benton

364 4 Jul 1831--Joseph Gordon to John Wiggens...$200...land Miles
Benton left to build schoolhouse, 2 acres on W and 1 3/4 acres on
E side of Edenton Rd; was sold to Gordon for taxes...
W.R. Riddick   Jos. Gordon
Alfred Ballard

365 5 Mar 1831--Mills Riddick, clerk of court, to Abram Morgan..
$5 for 20 acres, $7 for 3 acres and $3 for 5 acres adjoining his
own land and sold by court petition by Richard I. and Mary A. Gregory and others...
Jno.B.Baker   Mills Riddick
Law.L.Daughtry

366 10 May 1831--Solloman Ellis to Joshua Jones...$10...7 acres,
being part of a tract bought of Jethro Brinkley and wife, Sally,
on N side of Thicket Road adjoining land of Margaret A. Ballard
and said Jones...   Soloman(x)Ellis
Alfred Ballard
James Morgan

367 21 Nov 1831--Division of estate of Isaac Hunter and includes
two tracts: One 1117 acres and second one of 340 acres. Survey No.
1--Thomas Hunter...468 acres beginning at main road leading from
Hunters Mill to Sandy Cross NW to Hardy Easons line to line of Jacob
Walters heirs to Timothy Hunters to edge of swamp. No. 2--Isaac Hunter...649 acres beginning at road on edge of swamp to Hollow Bridge
in William Reed's line SE to a pine stump in Allen Brigg's line to

run of Kiledor Swamp and down swamp. Also, the 340 acres known as
Capt. Isaac Hunter's Plantation beginning at mouth of small branch
and running to corner of W. Harrells and NW to Mill Pond...

Jos. Gordon
Wm. Harrell
Jethro Ballard, surveyor   Thomas Twine

363 20 Sep 1828--Henry Gilliam and Mills Riddick release condit-
ional deed on tract of land whereon John Lewis lives, for which
they received as security for note, now canceled.

H. Gilliam
John Gatling   Mills Riddick

364 15 Aug 1831--Division of estate of Henry Walton including two
tracts of 523 acres 2 roods and 31 poles. Survey No. 1--Willis
Walton...115 acres 2 rds 27 po. beginning at edge of Catherine
Creek Swamp in run of Thompsons Swamp NW to edge of high ground in
Moses Hills line to Spring Branch. No. 2--Elisha Walton...137 acres
2 rds 27 po...beginning at pine at edge of road NE and SE. No. 3--
Asa Walton...126 acres 27 po...beginning at corner of Elisha's NW
to Spring Branch and along line of marked trees. No. 4--Daniel Wal-
ton...126 acres 2 rds 27 po. beginning at a maple at corner of Eli-
sha's to red oak at Virginia road NW to Jacob Walton's heirs to cor-
ner of Timothy Waltons and SE to Harrells fence. Also, 1 acre on
Chowan River at Old Town is given to said Elisha... Nathan Riddick
Jethro Barnes, surveyor   Reuben Nixon
Jethro H. Riddick, alternate   Timothy Walton
Joseph Riddick, alternate

369 25 Nov 1826--Jacob Powell to Charles Briggs...$500...65 acres
N side of Baylis Swamp beginning at mouth of branch, Ellis corner
tree NW to John C. Gordon's line to William Miller's line to Mills
Swamp and down to high water mark...   Jacob Powell
Jos. Gordon
Jas. Granbury

370 10 Feb 1827--James T. Freeman to John Cleaves...$22...5 acres
in Indian Neck beginning at small red oak in Clement Hill's line
SE to Isaac Lassiters...   Jas.T.Freeman
Mills(x)Eure
Isaac(x)Lassiter

371 25 Sep 1831--William, Thomas and John B. Walton, Nathan Nixon
and wife, Sarah, and Elizabeth, Timothy, Mildred, Mary Ann and Joseph Walton to Andrew Baker...$670...150 acres whereon George Freeman
now lives, which Timothy Walton received as security for debts...
David(x)Hobbs   Timothy Walton
Daniel Hobbs   Milly Walton

272 1 Nov 1831--Dempsey Eure and wife, Mary, to Nathaniel Eure...
$125...112 acres known as the Warren Land, which was heired by
Mary from her mother, beginning at sweet gum in Cypress Branch, a
corner of James Williams and Elisha Bonds NE to a line of Bonds,
formerly Henry Copelands, SE to red oak, a corner of Bonds, Richard Odom and heirs of Robert Warren, dec. to corner of heirs of
Robert and John Warren to line of said Williams, formerly Barnes...

Demsey Eure
Wills Cowper   Mary(x)Eure
Peter Eure

374 9 Jul 1831--Josiah Vaughan and wife, Abby, of Nansemond to Jordan Parker...$50...24 acres of undivided share of 74 acres formerly belonging to Alfred Parker, dec., brother of said Abby, which she heired from his estate and which was given to said Alfred by will of his grandfather, Thomas Parker, dec., adjoining lands of Tilly W. Carr, Kedar Ballard and others...

Jno.C.Gordon
Geo. Kittrell

Josiah Vaughn
Abigail(x)Vaughn

374 19 Jul 1831--Henry W. Skinner to Francis Bunchane...$40...3 acres in N part of Gatesville bounded on E by main street, S by Wright Hays lot, W by Henry Gilliam and N by said Skinner...

Jesse I. Cox
Micajah Riddick

Henry W.Skinner

375 1 Nov 1831--Francis Bunchane to Henry W. Skinner...$40...all rights in lot described in preceding deed...

Wm. Morse
Stuart Morse

Frs. Buchane

375 12 Apr 1831--Abram Beeman to daughter, Margaret Sparkman, wife of Dempsey Sparkman, gift of Negro girl, Edith...

Timothy Walton
Tinson Eure

Abm. Beeman

376 13 Feb 1832--Elisha Walton to Timothy Walton...$250...Negro woman, Ginny...

Walton Freeman

Elisha Walton

376 1 Aug 1831--John V. Sumner, sheriff, to John R. Norfleet...$1.89 in taxes for 1828...71 acres belonging to Jesse L. Hare, adjoining land of James Morgan and others and beginning at pine in road in Parker Jones line, along Jordon Parkers line and down run of Orapeak Swamp...excepting 1 acre...

Jas.C.Riddick
James Booth

John Sumner

377 1 Aug 1831--John V. Sumner, sheriff, to John R. Norfleet...$2.12 in taxes for 1828 on 71 acres belonging to Benjamin Blanchard beginning at stake of William Blanchards opposite Henry Bonds house NE to Pearce's line to Great Marsh NW to old corner of Benjamin Brown and Benbury Waltons SE to Easton Blanchards...

James Boothe
Jas.C.Riddick

John V. Sumner

378 21 Nov 1831--John R. Norfleet to Thomas Twine...$15...70 acres that he bought for 1828 taxes, described in preceding deed...

W. Riddick
Lassiter Riddick

Jno.R. Norfleet

379 31 May 1828--Henry Riddick to Sidney Hurdle...$240...Negro girl, Betty...

John Willey

Henry Riddick

380 18 Nov 1831--Blake Brady to Sidney Hurdle...$175...Negro boy, Kedar...

John Willey

Blake Brady

380 13 Apr 1831--Nancy, Isaac, Sarah, John, Elizabeth and Penninah
Parker to Mills Sparkman...$60...60 acres beginning at a stump at
foot of Fort Island in edge of outside pocosin running to Sparkman's
line to corner in pond, down pond to Mills Eure's line...

	Nancy(x)Parker	John Parker
John Willey	I.L. Parker	Elizabeth(x)Parker
Arthur Williams	Sarah(x)Parker	Penninah(x)Parker

381 11 Jun 1831--Nathaniel Eure, administrator of Lewis Eure, dec.
to Elizabeth Eure...$210.01...Negro man Tom...to pay debts...
Peter Eure   Nath'l Eure

381 30 Jul 1830--David Benton to Charles B. and Elbert W. Matthews,
his relations...gift of 307 acres, purchased recently from Joseph
Gordon, trustee of Ethel'd Matthews, adjoining lands of Tilly W.
Carr, Elbert having part where dwelling house stands...
Jno. O. Hunter   David(x)Benton
Abraham Riddick

382 30 Jul 1830--David Benton to Martha Jane, Mary and Lavinah Matthews, his relations...gifts as follows: Martha Jane...Negro man Charles, Mary...1 mare 10 hogs 2 feather beds and furniture 8 chairs 2
pine chests 1 bofat and furniture 1 desk and book 3 iron pots 1 dutch
oven 1 griddle and gridiron 1 trunk 1 looking glass 2 sets knives and
forks 1 horsecart and wheels 2 brass candlesticks 2 tubs and pails
tongs and shovel and apple mill, Levinia...1 feather bed and furniture.
Jno. O. Hunter   David(x)Benton
Abraham Riddick

382 25 May 1831--Tilly W. Carr to Kedar Ballard Sr...$500...lot
that was allotted to Alfred Ballard's wife in division of plantation
of Thomas Parker, dec., whereon said Alfred now lives, bounded on W
by heirs of said Alfred, S by David Benton, E by Jordon Parker, and
N by land sold to Kedar Taylor on Thicket Road...
Kedar Ballard   T.W. Carr

383 30 Sep 1831--Jesse Vann to Etheldred Cross...$35.16...110 acres
beginning at white oak, corner of said Vann, Jacob Odom and Elisha
Bond, to a corner of James Brady's to a dead white oak, a corner of
James Williams and Burrell Griffith's...
Wm.L.Boothe   Jesse Vann
Richard Odom

383 18 Oct 1831--Willis W., Andrew R. and Isaac L. Harrell to Will-
iam Harrell...$75...30 acres, their part of their brother, Henry
Harrell's land at head of Horsepool Swamp, adjoining lands of heirs
of William Creecy Jr., dec., Joseph Gordon and John G. Liles...
                                                 W.W. Harrell
Joseph Gordon   Andrew R.Harrell
Wm.H.Harrell   Isaac L.Harrell

384 20 Oct 1831--John W. Odom to James C. Smith of Nansemond...$25
water mill, pond and 2 acres of land adjoining Samuel Cross, heirs
of Benjamin Odom, dec. and formerly belonging to Col. Richard Barnes, with mill seat, and bought by John W. Odom from his heirs...
                                                 John Odom

Open Court

385 20 Oct 1831--William G. Daughtry to Mary H. Johnson...$50...34
acres on Bennetts Creek beginning at a small cypress, a corner of
Lot No. 8 in the division of land formerly belonging to Robert
Parker, dec. and now owned by Thomas Saunders, SW across an island
to creek swamp to black gum at Old Landing...   W.G. Daughtry
Jason Saunders, Law.S. Daughtry

385 11 Oct 1830--William E. Pugh, clerk, to John C. Gordon...$327
and $4 court charges...27 acres bounded on NW by lands of said Gor-
don, S by Thomas A. Small and E by desert...sold by petition of
James P. Small, Elizabeth Small, et al...   Wm.E.Pugh
J. Fowlkes
J.R. Riddick
David L. Swain, judge of supreme court

386 12 Jul 1831--Barnes Goodman to Moses Wilkins...$150...75 acres
adjoining lands of William Benton and William Parker...
Jno.T.Gary   Barnes Goodman
Thomas L.Gary

387 16 Aug 1831--Kedar Ellis is bound to Joseph Hanniford and Marmaduke N. Ellis...in order to settle controversy between said Kedar
and Hanniford in right of wife, Elizabeth, respecting settlement of
estate of John Ellis (they being his legal heirs) mutually choose
friends Henry Gilliam, Thomas Saunders, David Parker and Joseph
Gordon as arbitrators...   Kedar(x)Ellis
H. Gilliam

387 5 Oct 1831--Received of Marmaduke N. Ellis...$158.32 in full of
right of wife, Mary, from estate of Sarah N. Ellis...
                                                  Kedar(x)Ellis
T. Saunders
Jos. Gordon

387 5 Oct 1831--Joseph Hanniford to M.N. Ellis...$450...Negroes
Jack, Tom, Julia and children, Moses and Cynthia, and release all
claims to any slaves of estate of John Ellis and Sarah N. Ellis
and has received full share of wife's rights in slaves after death
of her mother and all slaves given her by her father, John Ellis,
after death of his widow, Mary Ellis...   Joseph Hanniford
Jos. Gordon

388 4 Oct 1831--Benjamin Brinkley to Marmaduke N. Ellis...$158.35
my rights of wife, Penelope in estate of Sarah N. Ellis...
                                                  Benjamin Brinkley
Jesse Wilson

388 10 Sep 1831--Humphrey Parker to Kedar Ellis...$22.63...in-
terest in Negroes Cate, Julia, Jack, Isaac, Tom and Moses...
H. Gilliam   Humphrey Parker

389 19 Aug 1830--Elisha R. Hunter to Timothy Hunter...$200...83
acres in Meherin Swamp adjoining lands of William Hunter's heirs,
Isaac Hunter's heirs, Frederick Jones and others... Elisha R. Hunter
J. Riddick
John Alpin

389 23 Feb 1831--James Baker to Thomas Twine...$105...500 acres

beginning at a marked cypress on Bennetts Creek W by dead junipers, through Juniper Swamp to Chowan River to Beef Creek E to Jacob Hinton's line...

James Baker

Reuben Clark
Abel Rogerson

390 27 Jul 1831--Charles Briggs to James Powell...$40...17 acres, part of tract where said Charles now lives, beginning at main public road in William Miller's line to edge of Mill Swamp and with Charles fence...

Charles Briggs

Jos. Gordon

390 4 Jul 1830--Arthur Gatling to John Riddick...$55...78 acres adjoining land of said Riddick, John B. Baker and others...

Arthur Gatling

Wm.L. Boothe
Peter Piland

391 20 June 1831--James Brinkley to Jesse Mathias...$50...300 acres, ½ of tract of marsh land on N side of White Oak Spanish Marsh, adjoining heirs of William Riddick, Col. Josiah Riddick, Mills Riddick and Miles Brinkley and is same land given by David Brinkley, dec. by will to James and Mills Brinkley and is yet undivided. For a more particular description see division of heirs of William Riddick and David Brinkley, dec...

James Brinkley

Demsey Vann
Jno. Brinkley

392 17 Feb 1827--Sarah Reed to Samuel Brown...$40...40 acres beginning at corner tree in Thomas Bagley's line, by a line of marked trees to John Morris line and down swamp to gum in John Roberts...

Benjamin Brown   Sarah (x) Reed
Elioner (x) Blanchard

292 10 Sep 1831--Henry Gilliam to Samuel Brown...$8.34...100 acres in Great Marsh, formerly property of Peter Boss and sold for taxes beginning at stake in Brown's line, a corner tree of Benbury Walton's SE to edge of meadow NW and then SE...

H. Gilliam

Benbury Walton
Jos. J. Barnes

393 10 Nov 1831--Benbury Walton to Samuel Brown...$35...190 acres in Great Marsh, formerly property of Peter Boss, and sold for taxes beginning at stake in Brown's line to Henry Gilliams and E to Pearces line and SE...

Benbury Walton

Benjamin Brown
Thomas Blanchard

394 7 Jul 1832--Parker Mitchell to William E. Pugh...$1.00 and to secure notes of said Mitchell and Jeptha Fowlkes...1 sorrell horse cart and gigg harness 2 feather beds and furniture bureau drawing table breakfast table set of china teaboard dozen plates 4 pitchers 1 dozen bowls 1 dozen tumblers household and kitchen furniture...

Parker(x)Mitchell
J. Fowlkes
Wm.E.Pugh

Henry R. Pugh

395 23 Dec 1831--Division of estate of Lewis Eure, including 9 tracts
of land valued at $2672.40, as follows: Survey No. 1--Mary Ann Eure...
Richard H. Lee tract of 75 acres, Mary Walters and William March
tracts of 46 acres, Daniel Rogerson tract of 54 acres and the John
Hyatt tract of 10 acres. No. 2--Henry Eure...Isaac Lee tract of 100
acres, tract where Elizabeth Lee now lives of 75 acres, being land
said Lewis drew in right of wife Elizabeth, daughter of Henry Lee,
and the Benjamin Rogers tract of 24 acres. No. 3--Armesia Eure...
George Gatling tract of 100 acres, part of house plantation tract
of 238 acres. No. 4--Mills Eure...part of house lot tract of 356
acres. No. 5--James Carter in right of wife, Emily Melissa...part of
house plantation of 406 acres in Beaverdam Swamp and adjoining for-
mer lines of Henry Speight, heirs of Henry Jones and others. Armesia
to Mary $11.48 and to Henry $4.24, Mills to Henry $40.12 and Melissa
to Henry $40.12 to make each one's share worth $534.48.

R. Gatling
John Willey
William Gatling,   John Saunders
alternate   Dempsey S. Goodman

397 7 Apr 1831--Miles M. Davis to Willis I. Riddick...$1.00 and to
secure bonds to John Walton...50 acres whereon Benjamin Blanchard
Sr. formerly lived and by him sold to Absolom Blanchard, who sold
to said Davis...adjoins lands of Samuel Brown and heirs of William
Blanchard, dec...

Miles M. Davis
Timothy Hays   J. Walton
Nathan Nixon   Willis I. Riddick

398 10 Mar 1831--John Cleaves of the first part, James T. Freeman,
second part and Willis I. Riddick, third part; whereas said Cleaves
is indebted to said Freeman for $45...for $1.00 and to secure payment...2 tracts in Indian Neck, which said Freeman sold to said
Cleaves and 8 acres of another tract said Freeman purchased of Isaac
Lassiter and then sold to said Cleaves, and 1 sorrel horse sow and
pigs household and kitcheon furniture...First tracts contain 5 acres.

John(x)Cleaves
John Walton   Jas.T.Freeman
John Roberts   Willis I.Riddick

399 21 Feb 1832--Wilie Riddick and wife, Eliza H., to John Roberts...
$258...64 acres 2 roods, all the lot that they drew in division of es-
tate of Mary Harrell, dec. beginning at white oak on main road along
road to Reuben Hintons SW to corner of Leah Hintons to head of Jacobs
Branch...

David Outlaw   W. Riddick
J. Walton   Eliza H. Riddick

400 6 Jul 1832--Parker Mitchell to John Bond and Benbury Walton...
$125...horsecart and gigg 2 bedsteads and beds dining table bureau
½ doz. chairs breakfast table set of china teaboard doz. glasses
candlestand and kitcheon furniture...

Parker(x)Mitchell
Lem. Cleaves
Wm.G.Daughtry

401 13 Dec 1831--Isaac Pipkin to Willis F. Riddick...$1200..4 acres
called the Grove in Gatesville beginning at road at middle of branch

at fork called Honey Pot Road leading to Bennetts Creek Branch
to nearly opposite corner of Jesse Browns lot to line of James
Garrett's heirs and Willis Parkers heirs...
Wm.H.Goodman   Isaac Pipkin

402 20 Feb 1832--Willis F. Riddick, trustee, to James Pruden of
Hertford...$50...150 acres devised to John Pruden by his father,
James Pruden, dec. and another tract of 12 acres known as the Jet-
hro Riddick Place, which was sold by virtue of a deed of trust,
adjoining land of David Riddick, John Matthews and others...
                                              Willis F. Riddick
David F. Felton

403 20 Feb 1832--Willis F. Riddick, trustee, to James Pruden of
Hertford...$138.30 by deed of trust...property of John Pruden:
sorrell mare and colt 3 feather beds and furniture buffet crockware
walnut table and chairs household, kitchen and dairy furniture 12
head cattle 33 head hogs 2 carts and wheels, Negro Charles and Negro
Diner crop of fodder apple and all other property...
David F. Felton   Willis F. Riddick

404 Feb Ct 1832--Abraham Beeman to daughter, Mildred...gift of
Negro girl, Ame...
Timothy Walton   Abrm.Beeman
Tinson J. Eure

405 12 Apr 1831--Abraham Beeman to daughter, Rachael, gift of Neg-
ro boy, Daniel...
Timothy Walton   Abrm.Beeman
Tinson J. Eure

405 20 Feb 1832--John Lewis to James Lassiter...$35...86½ acres or
½ of a tract, heired from his father, Mills Lewis, which formerly
belonged to said Mills and John Vann Sr. and Vanns part was purchased by William Gatling and from him by said Lassiter at a sheriff's
sale...lies near Honey Pot Pocosin...
                                                     Jno. Lewis
Jethro Barnes
Jno.D.Pipkin

406 Feb Ct 1832--Jno. B. Baker to Abraham Morgan...land, which
was held by deed of trust to secure notes to Jane A. Gregory (sub-
sequently Jane A. Hodges) now release 305 acres bounded by John
Duke on N and by run of Bennetts Creek on E and adjoining land belonging to Micajah Riddick and tract purchased by Richard B. Gregory from Noah Hinton, William S. Barnes and Abraham Morgan...
                                                   Jno.B.Baker
I. Riddick
P.B. Minton

407 5 Oct 1831--Marmaduke N. Ellis to Kedar Ellis...$10...Negro
woman Julia Boy Moses and Girl Sintha...
Jos. Gordon   Marmaduke N.Ellis

407 1 Oct 1831--Marmaduke N. Ellis to Kedar Ellis and wife, Mary...
$1.00 and for them to release all rights of dower to land sold to
Benjamin Brinkley known by name The Ridges containing 100 acres ad-
joining lands of Jesse Mathias, John Brinkley and others...
                                             Marmaduke N.Ellis
Demsey Vann
Benjamin Brinkley

407 1 Oct 1831--Marmaduke N. Ellis and Kedar Ellis and wife, Mary, to Benjamin Brinkley...$125...31 1/3 acres known by name White Oak Neck beginning at black gum in Orapeak Swamp, a corner tree of Esther and Elizabeth Ellis to William Matthias and down swamp...it being land Elizabeth Ellis heired from her father's estate and sold by her to her brother, John Ellis, 18 Oct 1804...
Demsey Vann
Jacob D. Bagley

Marmaduke N.Ellis
Kedar(x)Ellis
Mary(x)Ellis

408 25 Jan 1832--Robert Rogers, executor to the will of Jonathan Rogers, dec. whereas: said Jonathan departed this life sometime in 1830 and in his will asked that a certain tract of land be exposed to sell to pay any expenses...said Robert for $251.75 sells to Levi Rogers...109 acres on N side of Mills Swamp beginning at a corner white oak running SE to a gum at run of swamp to a white oak, James Jones corner thence on his line and Pipkin's line NE to a white oak, a corner and E to Old Path binding on path to branch SE...it being a tract purchased by said Jonathan in his lifetime of John Shepherd.

Dempsey S. Goodman
Jeptha Fowlkes

Robert Rogers, ex..

409 8 Feb 1832--Levi Rogers to Robert Rogers...$251.75...109 acres described in deed preceding...

J. Fowlkes
D.S. Goodman

Levi Rogers

409 26 Feb 1831--Henry Gilliam, trustee, to Thomas Saunders...$63 45 acres adjoining land of Benjamin Hays and others and whereon Richard Cross now lives. Conveyed by deed of trust...
Reuben Hinton
Jeptha Fowlkes

H. Gilliam

410 6 Dec 1831--Hillory Willey, attorney for Jonathan Parker of Tennessee, to Jonathan Williams...$200...150 acres beginning at overcup oak, a corner tree between Dempsey Parker and Jonathan Williams in swamp running a line of marked trees binding on said Dempsey and Ann Harvey's to a post oak to Kicheon Norfleets to a corner of Miles Parkers and Henry G. Williams NE to swamp and down run...it being tract where Jonathan formerly lived (well-known as Old Place)...
John Willey

Hillory Willey

411 4 Jan 1832--Mary Hudgins to Eli Worrell...$100...Negro Gilley 24 years old...

Mary(x)Hudgins

Abr.W.Parker
Lemuel E. Howell

411 13 Aug 1830--James R. Riddick to James A. Ballard...$51.58 land of John Brinkley sold at instance of Jesse Wilson and Benjamin Sumner (Henry Bond real plantiff)...adjoining Abraham Riddick, Benjamin Franklin and heirs of Elisha Brinkley...
Wm.W.Cowper
John Willey

J.R. Riddick

412 10 Jan 1831--Elisha Walton to Reuben Hinton...$250.16...117

acres beginning at gum corner of James Washington in Hintons line
SE to branch and Frederick Pearce's line to John Hares line in Maple
Branch and up branch...
Anthony Matthews   Elisha Walton
R. Matthews

413 24 Oct 1831--Timothy Walton to Noah Roundtree...$60...5 acres
in Indian Neck whereon Thomas Spivey lived, adjoining lands of said
Roundtree, Daniel Eure and others...
Soloman R.B.Walton   Tim. Walton
Maria Elliott

413 22 Dec 1831--John Saunders to Noah Roundtree...$150...34 acres
beginning at pine sapling NE along Outlaws line to Boar Swamp to
Bonds line...   John(x)Saunders
P.B. Minton
Tim. Walton

414 7 Aug 1831--James R. Riddick, sheriff, to Peter B. Minton...
$20.50...land of Thomas Powell, adjoining Charles Powell, John Out-
laws heirs and others and sold at instance of said Minton, William
D. Taylor and Miles Welch...   James R. Riddick
H. Gilliam
W.G. Daughtry

415 10 Jan 1831-David Benton to Rissop Rawls...$2150...two tracts
of land...1st of 250 acres in Bennetts Creek which was devised by
late James Barnes to his son, Joseph J., whereon John V. Sumners now
resides adjoining lands belonging to heirs of John Riddick, dec. and
land of Augustus and Seth R. Morgan and others. The 2nd tract of 300
acres is 4 undivided fifth parts of tract which said James Barnes
devised to son, Benjamin, which descended to his heirs John, William
S. and Joseph J. Barnes and Elizabeth Sumner, wife of John V. Sumner,
and said Benjamin Barnes...   David(x)Benton
James Morgan
James Costen

21 Jan 1832--James Benton to son, Seth, gift of 59 acre plantation,
where on said James lives bounded by lands of David Benton and heirs
of Edward Knight, dec...   James(x)Benton
James Morgan
John Taylor

416 4 Feb 1832--H.W. Skinner to Prior Savage...$40...3 acres on
street at corner of W. Hays and H. Gilliams N and down Skinners
line E to store at corner of Hays land...   H.W. Skinner

Jo. Riddick
Lem'l Cleaves

417 4 Feb 1832--H.W. Skinner to Jesse Brown...$50...5 acres be-
ginning at chopped gum at road at corner of John Brown's S and W
to Skinners line and H. Gilliams line...   H.W. Skinner
Jno. Bond
J. Walton

417 4 Feb 1832--H.W. Skinner to trustees of Lebanon Church...$10...

1/6 of an acre at corner of Wright Hays on Honey Pot Street and
running S...
Jno. Bond   H.W. Skinner
J. Walton

417 10 Nov 1830--Susanna Piland to Exum Lewis...$450...80 acres be-
ginning at gum on main road along John B. Bakers line to run of swamp
to William W. Cowper's line and along his line to road...
William L. Boothe   Susanna Piland
Wm.W. Cowper

417 1 Jan 1832--Reuben Hinton Sr. to Henry Pearce...farm let of
part of tract whereon he lives bounded by Nathaniel Jones, James
Trevathan and Noah Hinton...for 15 years for 1/3 production of
corn, peas, fodder, wheat and potatoes...
Sarah Pritchard   Reuben Hinton
B. Blanchard

419 1 Feb 1832--Bernard March to Francis Duke...$36.12½...14½ acres
beginning at a gum, corner of said March's in Gallbush Branch NE to
a pine and then E to Pearces Branch, down branch to state line...
                                                   Bernard March
William Lee

419 1 Feb 1832--William Lee to Francis Duke...$172...69 acres be-
ginning at pine called The Major in John March's line to Pearces
Branch up run and NW...
Open Court   William Lee

420 2 Dec 1831--Whitmill Hill to R.H. Parker...$200...26 acres be-
ginning at spanish oak, a corner in Thomas Rice's line SW to pine
to land of Moses Speight S and then NE to pine, corner tree of said
Rice and John Riddick...
Bn.B.Ballard   Whitmill Hill
Riddick Hunter

420 1 Dec 1831--Richard H. Parker to Robert Hill...$250...57 acres
beginning at persimmon tree in a small branch on Sumners line SE to
post oak, Eason's corner along line NW to edge of swamp SW to holly
near pine stump and up swamp to mouth of branch...
Bn.B.Ballard   Rich'd H. Parker
Riddick Hunter

421 2 Jan 1832--James Benton Sr. and Seth Benton Jr. to John P.
Benton...$600...Negroes Siller, Dick, Cate, Abram and Cherry...
William Powell   Jas.(x)Benton
Brian Hare   Seth(x)Benton
John Wiggens

421 4 Jan 1832--John Arnold to John P. Benton...$17...8 acres ad-
joining land of Tilly W. Carr and others...
John Wiggens   John Arnold
Wm.W.Powell

422 19 Sep 1832--Dempsey Eure to Samuel Eure...$1.00 and to se-
cure notes of $989.71 and $23.47 to Abram W. Parker...land adjoin-

ing John Beeman, dec., said Parker, James Brown and others and
whereon said Dempsey lives containing 200 acres and Negroes Jim
and Mary...

Elisha Parker
William Carter

Demsey Eure
A.W. Parker
Sam'l Eure

423 21 May 1832--Tinson Eure to Samuel Eure...$1.00 and to secure
note to Abram W. Parker for $266.98...100 acres beginning at black
gum in branch near road down road to corner red oak in Jethro Eure's
line to John Beeman's line to corner of Beemans and Asa Harrells
along Harrells line to paw paw gum in edge of Coles Creek and up
creek to Deep Branch...

Elisha Parker
William Carter

Tinson Eure
A.W. Parker
Sam'l Eure

424 4 Jan 1832--John Arnold to John P. Benton...$100...10 acres
adjoining land formerly belonging to James Benton and others it
being all the land said Arnold owns on W side of main road from
Wiggens Crossroads to Elm Swamp...

John Wiggens
Wm.W. Powell

John Arnold

424 18 Feb 1832--George Costen to Frederick Hinton...$800...160
acres beginning at mouth of Juniper Branch up branch to bridge
called Aaron Blanchard's Bridge to gum on branch and binding on
Thomas Garretts and down branch to Catherine Creek...

B. Blanchard
R. Blanchard

George Costen

425 5 Jan 1832--Frederick Hinton to George Costen...$600...90 acres
beginning on main road binding on James Boothes line along Reuben
Hinton's line to corner white oak along John Roberts line to Leah
Hinton's line to corner white oak along line to main road...

B. Blanchard
R. Blanchard

Frederick Hinton

425 5 Jan 1832--Joseph Gordon to John Alpin...$1800...290 acres,
part of land formerly belonging to Moses Briggs and by his last
will lent to Abraham Harrell and wife, Mary, during their lives
and then given to Moses B. Harrell, joining lands of Joseph Riddick, William Harrell and others...

Marmaduke Norfleet
Thomas Jones

Joseph Gordon

426 11 May 1831--James Carter to Mrs. Penelope Carter...$306...
Negro Man Reuben...

J.R. Riddick

James Carter

426 11 May 1831--Thomas S. Spivey to William Moore $500...Negroes
Peggy, Cynthia, Soloman and Cacey...

Jno.R. Gilliam

Abram Morgan

427 6 Mar 1832--James Williams to James R. Riddick...to secure note
of $221 to John Figg...Negroes Cherry and children, Lewis and Benjamin

Wm.W. Riddick

James Williams
J.R. Riddick

428 8 May 1832--Richard H. Ballard to James Morgan...$1.00 and to
make safe debt to David Benton...250 acres called Folly Plantation
whereon he lives adjoining John C. Gordon and others...
Jesse Wiggens   R.H. Ballard
Wm.W.Powell

429 25 Aug 1832--Nathaniel Jones to John Walton, trustee...$1.00
and to secure note to John Roberts for $150...40 acres whereon he
lives adjoining Reuben Hinton, James Trevathan, John Jones and George
Freeman; 3 feather beds and furniture, 3 head cattle, 10 hogs, all
household and kitchen furniture, crops of corn, fodder, peas and potatoes now growing...
                                                 Nathaniel(N)Jones
Benbury Walton   John Roberts
Jno. Bond   John Walton

430 22 Dec 1831--Whereas marriage is intended between Benjamin
Blanchard and Judith Lewis; said Judith to sell in trust to Riddick Blanchard for $50...parcel of land whereon she lives, 2 feather
beds and furniture, 1 desk, 3 tables, dozen chairs, 2 pots, 1 Dutch'
oven, 1 heifer, 1 sow and pigs, 1 looking glass, parcel of crockery,
loom and gear... to hold in trust...   B. Blanchard
J. Walton   Judith Lewis
Easton Blanchard   R. Blanchard

431 10 Dec 1831--William G. Daughtry to William Ely...$800...lot
in Gatesville beginning at ditch, down line of Micajah Reeds running
SE on main street then NE...
Ro. Riddick   W.G. Daughtry
Pryer Savage

432 21 Jan 1832--E.P. Akerman and wife, Susannah, to Exum Jenkins
$400...lot set apart from original of 210 acres to Susannah in div-
ision of Francis Speight, dec. bounded by land of Robert Saunders,
dec.(now Gilbert Saunders, Ann Speight, Sarah Saunders and Jenkins...
                                                  E.P. Akerman
John W. Darden   Susanna Akerman
Willis L. Woodley
Edward Howell

432 6 Mar 1832--Charles Williams to James R. Riddick...$137...70
acres on S side of Bennetts Creek, it being part of tract whereon
James Cross formerly lived and died, which Richard Cross heired by
death of his father, James, and sold to said Williams...begins at
main road leading from Gatesville to Sunsbury at Hollow Bridge in
Hilly Tree Branch up branch to David Parkers line...
                                                  Charles Williams
Ro. Riddick
J. Walton

433 18 May 1832--Richard H. Ballard to William W. Stedman...$10...2
acres beginning at red oak near road and NW...
John Hofler   R.H. Ballard

434 1 Jan 1831--James T. Freeman to David Outlaw...$5...undivided
interest in 50 acre tract whereon Miles Roundtree formerly lived...
P.B.Minton   Jas.T.Freeman
M. Hudgins

434 21 Feb 1832--Thomas B. Hunter to Thomas Riddick of Perquimans
$4500...527 acres bounded on N by main road, SE by Hardy Eason, W
by Meherin Swamp and on S by lands of Jacob Walton, Timothy Hunter
and John Hunter...it being same tract formerly belonging to Isaac
Hunter...   Thos.B.Hunter
George Costen
Wm.S.Cowper

435 24 Nov 1831--Andrew Baker to Burwell Brothers...$250...27 acres
where he formerly lived and purchased of Timothy Walton and Henry
Spivey, adjoining lands of David Hobbs, Timothy Walton and Walton
Freeman...   Andrew Baker
Jos. Gordon
A.R. Harrell

435 1 Apr 1831--Drew M. Saunders to Jason Saunders...$275...186
acres beginning at marked water oak on Deep Cypress Swamp to corner
of James Williams, down swamp to corner of Elizabeth Lee's...
G.G.Saunders   Drew M. Saunders
John Speight

436 1 Mar 1832--Cyprian R. Cross to Etheldred Cross...$800...300
acre plantation, which his father, Abraham Cross, dec. gave him in
his will...on N side of Cypress Swamp beginning at road which leads
from Richard Odoms to Winton at place where land commences, which
Cyprean Cross gave in his will to Riddick Cross and said Riddick sold
to Taylor Cross, thence with line to land belonging to heirs of Taylor Cross, to Jacob Odom's line to land belonging to heirs of Benjamin Barnes, dec. to corner of Craffords land thence to John R. Norfleet's line (formerly Odoms) to Beemans line to road...
Rich. Odom   Cyprian R. Cross
T. Saunders

437 21 Nov 1831--Mills Sparkman to David Umphlet...$47.50...29 acres
SW side of Cypress Swamp beginning at Levi Eure's line at mouth of
branch on swamp S to Peter Harrells and along his line back to swamp.
Thos. Hoggard   Mills Sparkman
Samuel Green

437 23 Oct 1827--Dempsey Langston of Nansemond to John Langston...
$500...172 acre tract of land bought from Jno V. Sumner, at sheriff's
sale...adjoining lands of Elizabeth Lee, Lewis Eure, and heirs of
Brian Saunders, dec...   Dempsey Langston
John A. March
Willis(x)Parker

438 15 Dec 1831--George Brooks to daughter, Martha S. Melvin...gift
of 88 acres of land on Watery Swamp at end of her ditch, a corner of
Joseph Brooks, running down main road to gum nearly SW by line of
marked trees to pine, a corner tree in Samuel Brown's line, along his
line to said Joseph's and E back to said ditch...   George Brooks
J. Walton
James(x)Lassiter

438 15 Dec 1831--George Brooks to daughter, Ann E. Lassiter...gift of
88 acres on Watery Swamp beginning at sweet gum, corner tree on Margaret C. Brooks line to a pine, another corner in Brown's line nearly

NW to a water oak and NE by line of marked trees to Swamp to a
sweet gum, a corner on Henry Hoflers and up swamp...
J. Walton   George Brooks
James(x)Lassiter

439 15 Dec 1831--George Brooks to son, Joseph...gift of 88 acres on
Watery Swamp beginning at a gum stump, a corner on Thomas Twine's
down swamp by ditch to Martha S. Melvins S and then E...
J. Walton   George Brooks
James(x)Lassiter

440 15 Dec 1831--George Brooks to daughter, Martha C...gift of 88
acres beginning at black gum in Watery Swamp on Martha S. Melvin's
SW to corner of Ann E. Lassiters and up swamp...
J. Walton   George Brooks
James(x)Lassiter

441 15 Dec 1831--Martha S. Melvin, John Lassiter and wife, Ann E.,
Joseph Brooks and Margaret C. Brooks to George Brooks and wife, Sally,
all rents and farm let of land, containing 351 acres, whereon George
and Sally now live and which he divided amongst his children by deed
15 Dec. 1831. Land was purchased by said George from Amos Smith 1 Aug
1792 and begins at sweet gum in Watery Swamp up run to corner tree in
Dempsey Blanchard, dec. line NE to a nole, thence SE to head of branch to a corner tree in Henry Harrell, dec. line in swamp...
                              Margaret C. Brooks Martha S. Melvin
J. Walton   George Brooks   John(x)Lassiter
James(x)Lassiter   Sally(x)Brooks   Ann E.Lassiter
                                                  Joseph Brooks

442 25 Feb 1832--Lucy Walton to William Walton...$150...all rights
of dower laid off to her by courts of land of her late husband, Timothy Walton, dec...
A. Blanchard   Lucy Walton
Timothy Walton

442 20 Mar 1832--James Goodman and Benjamin Riddick of Nansemond
to Nathan Cullens...$1000...303 acres on E side of Catherine Creek
adjoining lands of Robert Taylor, dec., Nathan Nixon, Hance Hofler
and others; it being land that formerly belonged to William Freeman
and sold by him to Daniel Riddick, dec....
Jet.H.Ballard   James Goodman
Kindred Parker   Benja.Riddick

443 20 Feb 1832--John Langston to Willoughby Manning...$80...100
acres on Hilly Swamp adjoining land of John Norfleet, Jonathan Williams, Kicheon Norfleet and others...
Reuben Lassiter   John Langston
Joshua Jones

443 9 Jan 1832--Richard Bond to William Bond...$25...10 acres bound-
ed by James Costen and Samuel S. Bond; it being all the portion of
land he heired from his father, Richard Bond...
Reuben Hinton Jr.   Richard(x)Bond

443 14 May 1832--Noah Roundtree to John Saunders (of colour)...$20
6 acres beginning at black gum in run of branch SE and then N...
Nathan Nixon   Noah Roundtree
Jonathan Lassiter

443 15 Dec 1831--Mary Matthews to sister, Martha Jane, gift of 3
feather beds and furniture, 8 flayed bottom chairs, 2 pine tables,
1 bofat and its furniture, pine chest, desk and parcel of books, 3
iron pots, 1 dutch oven, gridiron and griddle, 1 trunk, 1 chest, 2
brass candlesticks, 2 pair fire tongs, 1 looking glass and all hogs.
Demsey Knight   Mary Matthews
Ethel'd Matthews

444 13 Mar 1832--James Williams to his daughter and son-in-law,
Sophia and Joshua Allen...gift of Negro girl, Lucinda...
Lem'l Riddick   James Williams
J.R. Riddick

445 18 Feb 1832--Arthur Jenkins and Ann Grant, who plan marriage,
agree all money and choices of action of said Ann be secured agree
to Elisha Bond as trustee...$1.00 to said Ann, who conveys the foll-
owing to said Bond: 4 cows, horse cart and wheels, 9 hogs, 3 beds
and furniture, household and kitchen furniture...
John Willey   Ann(x)Grant
Eff(x)Lewis   Arthur(x)Jenkins
                                                     Elisha H. Bond

447 6 Jan 1832--John W. Odom to Richard Alstin...$28.12½...11¼ acres
beginning at red oak in branch, corner of James Boothe and Jesse
Arline SW to a pine and NE to Arline's line...
Edwin Smith   John W. Odom
Richard T. Odom

447 1 Aug 1831--James Baker Sr to James Baker Jr...$60...150 acres
in Juniper Swamp between Catherine Creek and Bennetts Creek beginning at old cross roads to old ferry to edge of junipers to old canal
road...
Jet.H.Riddick   James Baker
Abel Rogerson

448 1 Mar 1832--William Goodman to Benjamin Eure...$32.50...50
acres beginning at pine and running Mills Eure's line to Great
Branch to corner oak of William Harrells to main pocosin...
John Langston   William Goodman
Jethro Teabout

448 1 Mar 1832--William Goodman to Jethro Teabout...$45...50 acres
beginning at pine on river pocosin, a corner tree of Mills Eures down
river to heirs of John Roundtree to head of Thick Neck Branch to a
gum in Little Cosse Branch formerly corner of James Bradys and said
Eure's line; being patent to John Rawls Jr. 1 Apr 1723...
John Langston   William Goodman
Benjamin Eure

449 10 Oct 1830--Jethro Eure Sr. to son, Levi...gift of 50 acres
of plantation whereon said Levi lives on E side of road from White
Oak to Sarum Creek Landing...
Wm. L. Boothe & Samuel Eure   Jethro(x)Eure

449 20 Aug 1830--Miley Tooley to Jesse Mathias...$200...23 acres
bounded by lands of Jno.V.Sumner, Kedar Ellis and said Mathias...
Jas.A. Ballard   Miley Tooley
Riddick Jones

450 16 Mar 1832--William Hofler to Henry Bond...$211.55...116
acres beginning at corner gum at head of Dam Branch in Frederick

Hintons line along Hance Hoflers line to Indian Swamp to a gum in Abraham Morgans to Isaac Hoflers in Deep Branch to said Bonds.
N. Nixon
Jas.T.Freeman
William Hofler

450 1 Nov 1831--Susan Wolfrey to John Willey...$9...3 acres adjoining said Willeys purchase of John Riddick and beginning in line between said Susan and Willey SW to main road leading from Manneys Ferry to Gates Courthouse and down road...
H.H.C.Jones
Lewis I. Hurdle
Susan(x)Wolfrey

451 30 Jan 1833--Robert Simon to David Parker...50 cents...and to insure debt of $40...2 beds and furniture, 2 wheels, pot, kettle, dutch oven and skillet, 4 chairs, 1 dozen plates, 3 dishes, desk, 4 books, sow and 7 pigs, 5 dogs and pot trammel, 3 axes, hoe, 10 chickens, 2 chests, 2 tables, 2 water pails and tub, 1 barrell soap and 2 lbs. bacon...
James Parker
Robert Simons

452 18 Jun 1831--Rizop Rawls to Noah Harrell...$900...151½ acres on W side of Bennetts Creek beginning at a post oak near road, a corner tree in said Harrells NW to Moses Pocosin SE to James Lassiters and along his line to main road...
Sam'l R. Harrell
R. Rawls

453 6 May 1832--William D. Pruden to Elbert Riddick...$235...48 acres bounded on N by Celia Pruden, S by James M. Riddick, E by Abraham Morgan and W by David Riddick; cornering in Middle Swamp at tree of Riddick Matthews and James M. and David Riddick; same land set apart of said William D. in division of land of Nathaniel Pruden, dec...
H. Gilliam
David Riddick
Wm.D.Pruden

453 27 Feb 1832--George Costen to Thomas R. Costen...$600...land purchased at a court sale by Frederick Hinton Jr. and sold to said George beginning at fork of main road at James Boothes line to Reuben Hintons line to John Roberts and Leah Hintons and to road...
James Costen
Mary Fields
George Costen

454 19 Jan 1832--Elijah Hare of Nansemond to Gilbert G. Saunders $361.12...221 acres adjoining Miles Parker, heirs of Henry Jones dec. and others. Land was conveyed by Joshua Lang to said Hare as trustee to cover debts and whereas debts have not been paid, said Hare as trustee for James Hare and William Faulk, representing Henry Hare Sr., conveys to said Saunders...
Henry Carter
Myles Parker
Elijah Hare

455 11 May 1832--Mary Butler to Gilbert G. Saunders $32...9 acres conveyed to her by Micajah Reed, who purchased it at a sheriff's sale for taxes. bounded by said Saunders, Miles Parker and heirs of Lewis Eure, dec....
H.H.C.Jones
James Williams
Mary(x)Butler

455 16 Jan 1832--David Outlaw to William W. Hays...$467...163 acres
on S side of Catherine Swamp adjoining lands of Peter B. Minton, John
Mitchell, heirs of Thomas Hobbs, dec., Whitmill Stallings, Frederick
Rooks and John Saunders; being part of a tract whereon Miles Round-
tree, dec. formerly lived and died...
J. Walton   David Outlaw
Robert Williams

456 20 Jan 1830--John P. Cross of Sumner Co,Tn. appoints Soloman
K. Volentine as his attorney to convey 45 acres, which was allotted
to him by his late father, John Cross, whereon he lived and died...
Elijah Boddie, acting jp   John P. Cross
for Sumner Co.
Alfred H. Douglas & Thomas Anderson
certified

456 4 Mar 1830--Soloman Volentine of Sumner Co., Tn. agent for John
P. Cross, to William Cross...$135...45 acres adjoining lands of
Hillory Willey, Hardy Cross, Margaret Cross.
Jonathan Williams   Soloman Volentine
Demsey Goodman

457 8 Aug 1832--Kedar Green and wife, Judith, to Benbury Walton...
$50...90 acres individed land, which descended to Judith by death
of her father, Abner Pearce, adjoining lands of said Walton, Samuel Brown and Jethro Blanchard...
                                                     Kedar(x)Green
                                                     Judith(x)Green

458 3 Apr 1832--Richard Riddick and wife, Margaret, of Nansemond to
William H. Goodman...$360...Lot No. 1 of a tract of land devised a-
mong heirs of Henry Copeland, dec., on W side of Peters Swamp be-
ginning in road leading from Isaac Pipkins to William M. Harveys
NE to run of swamp, Nancy Parkers line to mouth of branch and E.B.
Gatlings corner...
                                                     Richard Riddick
Edw'd L. Neal   Margaret Riddick

459 19 Sep 1831--Elisha Walton to Whitmill Stallings...$204.24
Negro woman Jiney and child Milbrey...
Frederick Rooks   Elisha Walton

460 1 Jul 1832--Timothy Walton to John Alpin...$13.88...291 acres
formerly belonging to Moses Briggs, dec. and which he lent to Abraham Harrell and wife, Mary, for life and then to go to their son,
Moses B. Harrell.
Hillory Willey   Timothy Walton

459 28 Jun 1831--John V. Sumner, sheriff, to Timothy Walton...$13.88
291 acres belonging to Abraham Harrell and wife, Mary, for son, Moses
B.Harrell, for payment of 1828 taxes; beginning at Williams Harrells
corner SE to Joseph Riddicks to public road, to Abraham Pearces, to
Little Branch, to desert NW to Mills Riddicks...
David Parker   John V. Sumner

460 21 Feb 1832--Elisha H. Bond to Isaac Pipkin...$216...54 acres on
E side of road from Somerton to Winton, formerly belonging to William
Gatling Sr., know known by name Bonds Plantation, beginning at post

oak in Pipkin's line SE and NE to William H. Goodmans...
John Saunders   Elisha H. Bond
John Gatling
5 Mar 1832--Henry Bond to Isaac Pipkin $1.00...relinquish all in-
terest in land in preceeding deed...
                                                     Henry Bond

462 20 Aug 1832--John A. March of Nansemond and Jason Saunders to
Miles Parker...$400...70 acres, 2 tracts; first known as Sand Banks
beginning at Francis Rogers line, along his line to Jethro Sumners to Henry Hares, dec. to William Beasley's line to Chowan River
at Stoney Landing and down river to Gut Landing along Ira Odoms line
to Hares and Parkers. Second tract called Beasleys begins at gum
in Deep Cypress at Gilbert G. Saunders NE to said Parkers and NW...
Jethro Barnes   Jason Saunders
John Speight   John A. March
T. Saunders

463 14 Mar 1832--Etheldred Cross to Thomas Saunders...$275...Negro
girl Charlotte 15 years old...
                                                     Ethel'd Cross
Rich'd Odom
Cyprian R. Cross

463 17 Aug 1832--Henry Riddick to Robert Riddick Sr...$1700...170
acres beginning at lightwood post in Edward R. Hunters on W side of
road from Suffolk to Edenton E across road to corner of Edward Briggs,
Robert and Henry Riddick to Hollow Bridge NW; same land he purchased
of Robert Riddick Sr. and Isaac R. Hunter...
Jo. Riddick   Henry Riddick
David F. Felton

464 17 Aug 1832--Henry Riddick to Robert Riddick Sr...$1250...Negroes
London, Ben, Mary, Emmy, Lovey and her children, Edmond and Andrew,
and Chloe and her husband, Dempsey...
                                                     Henry Riddick
Jo. Riddick
David F. Felton

464 2 Jun 1832--Elisha Walton to Peter B. Minton...$20...1 acre be-
ginning in Old Town near creek and then NW...
Jethro H. Riddick   Elisha Walton
Abel Rogerson

465 17 Aug 1832--Elizabeth Lee to Nathaniel Eure...$400...187 acres
in Cypress Swamp, which she heired from her father, Isaac Pipkin Sr.,
being part of the King Tract beginning at an ash to Langs line (now
Gilbert Saunders) NE to John Speights and heirs of Charity Barnes,
now Eures line SW and down swamp...
William Lee   Elizabeth Lee
Dempsey S. Goodman

466 Nov Ct 1832--Elisha H. Bond to John Willey...$1.00 and to make
safe to Nathaniel Eure as security for $180 in notes to Robert Rogers,
Miles Parker, Jonathan Williams, Robert R. Smith, William Lee and
John H. Wheeler, all in hands of Jethro Willey...25 hogs, 10 head of
cattle, 2 yoke of oxen and 142 acres beginning at corner of Jacob
Odoms on line of Ben. Barnes to corner of Odoms and Jesse Vanns to
Richard Odoms...
                                                     Elisha H. Bond
                                                     John Willey
Jethro Willey   Nath'l Eure
Lemuel S. Powell

467 18 Jun 1832--Elisha Walton to James Baker...$150...137 acres
joining lands of Henry King, Willis Walton and others that he drew
in division of his fathers estate...
Abraham Twine   Elisha Walton
Wynns Baker

467 20 Oct 1830--Henry W. Skinner to Wright Hays...$34.33 1/3...
2 3/4 acres beginning at post on Honey Pot St. NW to a stone and
then SW to A. Parker's corner to church yard and then SE...
Lawrence S. Daughtry   H.W. Skinner
John S. Roberts

468 8 Jun 1832--Joseph Gordon to Nathan Ward...$1.00 and to secure
$500...notes to Thomas Twine made in 1830...50 acres conveyed to him
by deed of trust from said Ward...joining Jethro H. and Josiah Riddick.
Marmaduke Norfleet   Jos. Gordon
John Alpin

468 2 Aug 1832--William W. Stedman to Andrew Matthews...$62...62
acres purchased of James P. Small 16 Nov 1826...
R.H. Ballard   Wm.W.Stedman
Robert H. Ballard

469 26 Jul 1832--Soloman Eason to son, Reuben...gift of 100 acres
whereon Reuben lives, W side of Dismal Swamp to Willis Riddicks...
Jos. Gordon   Soloman(x)Eason
Mary G. Gordon

469 26 Jul 1832--Soloman Eason to son, Andrew...gift of 56 3/4 acres
whereon Andrew lives, bought of Jesse Pearce, adjoining Nathan Ward,
Joseph Riddick, formerly Isaac Riddick's, dec. and Josiah Riddick...
Jos. Gordon   Soloman(x)Eason
Mary G. Gordon

470 12 May 1832--Richard Odom to Demsey Parker...$35...41 acres be-
ginning at white oak, a corner of Henry Willeys, running his line to
Mary Parker's line to corner maple of Kicheon Norfleets to Levin Cuff.
Myles Parker   Rich'd Odom
William Cross

471 Aug Ct 1832--James R. Riddick, sheriff, to Jonathan Williams...
79¢ in taxes due for 1832...10 acres belonging to John Cross,dec.,
beginning at gum in Long Branch SW to Edwin Cross'   J.R. Cross
Simon Walters
Lassiter Riddick

471 14 May 1832--Prudence Williams to Jethro Barnes...$330...70
acres on E side of Suffolk Road in Mills Rogers line to Long Branch
up branch to late John Odom's line to run of Beech Swamp...
E. Smith   Prudence Williams
John W. Odom

472 24 Jul 1832--Garret Hofler to John Hinton Sr...$22.50...5 acres
beginning at gum in John Walton's line in Mirey Branch to marked pine
corner of Richard Blanchard and SE...
Jas. T. Freeman   G. Hofler
W. Hinton

473 23 Jun 1831--Sally Williams to children: Allen, Lavinia, Martha

and Robert Williams...Negro woman, Moriah and her child, Leah...
John Walton   Sally(x)Williams

473 26 Dec 1831--David Outlaw to John Saunders...$150...100 acres
N side of road leading from Whitmill Stallings to Peter B. Mintons
beginning at old road Frederick Rooks line to Simon Stallings...
Nathan Cullens   David Outlaw
Henry Bagley

474 9 Jan 1832--Willis I. Riddick to Samuel Ward...10 acres for
10 years and 1/3 of farm produce, beginning at dividing line between said Riddick and James W. Riddick, dec. and is place where
Jethro Reed formerly lived...
                                                Willis I. Riddick

474 3 June 1825--Whereas Daniel Williams sold to William Babb 23
acres for $57.50, adjoining lands of John H. Haslett, heirs of Win-
burn Jenkins, dec., heirs of William Babb, dec. 13 Feb 1826 and another
deed to Marmaduke Baker of 300 acres for $700 appears to cover land
in the first deed.. therefore to avoid further trouble said Marmaduke
for $1.00 releases all claim to said Babb land...   Marmaduke Baker
Blake Baker
H.G. Williams

475 2 Nov 1831--Division of 3/4 tract called John Fontains 6000,
belonging to Willie McPherson and heirs ; Mary Virginia Proctor,
daughter of Elizabeth B. and Samuel Proctor, dec. Said tract was
purchased by said McPherson from Richard Morris Sr. and sold one
undivided half to Samuel Proctor and Frederick B. Sawyer and said
Sawyer's part descended to his daughter, Elizabeth B. Survey No.
1 Swamp lands of Samuel Proctor to John I. Old, William Old, Thomas
B. Grissom and wife, Lovey, Simon Norman and wife, Elizabeth, Francis
Old, Louisa B. Old, Hollowell Old and James Old and Survey No. 2--
tract adjoining swamp to Samuel Proctor heirs...
                          David Prichard   MMC Sanderlin
                          Phineas Sanborn   Morgan Cartwright
                                             John Spence

478 10 May 1826--Division of estate of Williams Brothers: Survey No.
1--Julia Brothers...44 acres beginning at Mill Race to head line and
Sarah Davis house to Mill Dam. No. 2--Burrell Brothers...34 3/10
acres beginning at Mill Race SW to head line and NE to desert. No. 3---
James Brothers...26 acres beginning on side of desert SW to head
line. No. 4--Nancy Brothers...37½ acres beginning at desert and NE.
No. 4--Robert Brothers...37 1/8 acres beginning at corner of desert
SW to head line and NE. No. 6--Richard Brothers...37 1/8 acres be-
ginning at side of desert and SW. No. 7--James Baker in right of
wife, Esther, beginning at side of desert to Luke Greens corner...
                                             John C. Gordon
                                             Wm.W. Stedman
John Bouge, surveyor   William Harrell
Abraham Harrell, alternate

479 4 Jul 1832--Reuben Hinton to David Parker...50¢...Negroes
Grace, Eley, Margaret and Miles, already in his possession...
W. Hinton   Reuben Hinton
Burwell Brothers

479 4 Jul 1832--Hance Hofler to David Parker...$560.35...Negro,
Isaac...
H. Gilliam   Hance Hofler

479 2 Oct 1832--William Sears to Nancy Parker...$326...Negroes,
David and Emmy...
John Willey   William Sears

480 18 Feb 1833--Willie McPherson to Mills Riddick of Nansemond...
$600...400 acres of swamp land beginning at Gates and Camden county
lines NW to Mills and Josiah Riddicks and along canal; being part of
John Fontaines 6000 acres...
Jas. N. McPherson   W. McPherson

480 24 Dec 1827--Ann N. Harvey to John Roberts...$1250...4 Negroes,
Abram and wife, Rachael and 2 young children, Amey and Arrenetta...
J.R. Riddick   Ann N. Harvey

480 19 Nov 1832--Robert Parker and wife, Louisa, and Frederick
Morris to Timothy Walton...$70...91 acres that Robert and Louisa
drew in division of land of her father, Jesse Brown, dec. beginn-
ing at sweet gum, a corner of Timothy Waltons on old road SW to
William Browns to persimmon tree, corner of Sarah Browns...
                                                    Robert(x)Parker
Tho. L. Gary   Louisa(x)Parker
                                                    Frederick(x)Morris

481 30 Mar 1832--Miles Parker and wife, Martha, and Thomas Saunders
to Robert R. Smith of Nansemond and Benjamin Saunders...$30...10
acres and Copeland's Fishery, sometimes called Gutt Landing and now
known by name Lumberton, on Chowan River bounded by river, said Parkers and heirs of Henry Hare, dec...
                                                    Myles Parker
John Langston   Martha Parker
Henry Carter   Thomas Saunders

482 9 Feb 1832--Starkey Eure to James and Daniel Eure...20 acres
on Bennetts Creek to hold as security for loan...   Starkey Eure
Henry Jocelin
James Outlaw

482 23 Apr 1833--Isaac Lassiter to Starkey Eure...$120...20 acres
on E side of Bennetts Creek beginning at post oak, corner of Clement
Hills W to corner of Parkers SE and then NE...
James Outlaw   Isaac(x)Lassiter
Henry B. Lassiter

483 14 Dec 1826--James Powell to William W. Stedman...$52...21
beginning at pine stump at road leading to Holloday Waltons NW to
Powells and Stedmans corner in Folly Plantation to Ballards to
John Powells and back to road...
R.H. Ballard   James Powell
John Hoffler

483 13 Nov 1832--John W. Parker and Augustus Morgan of Nansemond to
Abraham Morgan...$400...200 acres ½ of land known as Dukes Tract be-
ginning at pine on E side of line tree between said land and Wills
Cowper W to Bennetts Creek, down creek and S to Rizop Rawls along
his line to Elizabeth Granburys NE to road and across road...
David Speight   Augustus Morgan
James Goodman   John W. Parker

484 13 Nov 1832--Augustus Morgan and John W. Parker of Suffolk to
Abraham Morgan...Negro man, Gilbert, about 25...
                                  Augustus Morgan
James Goodman   John W. Parker

484 8 Oct 1832--Thomas Twine to Abel Rogerson...$130...50 acres
beginning at marked cypress in Bennetts Creek W through Juniper
Swamp to Chowan River and up river to Beef Creek, up prong E to
Jacob Hintons and back to Bennetts Creek...
Burwell Brothers   Thomas Twine

485 4 Jan 1832--John W. Odom to James C. Smith of Nansemond...$80
80 acres beginning at pine in branch and SW up Mill Pond to James
Boothes, SE to corner of Boothes and Jesse Arline...
Willis L. Woodley   John W. Odom

485 11 Oct 1832--Jesse Matthias to John Taylor...$130...74 acres
joining Demsey Knight, John Barnes and said Taylor and land which
formerly belonged to Brinkley Henderson, who sold to said Matthias.
John Wiggens   Jesse Matthias
Jno.P.Benton
John Barnes

486 1 Oct 1832--Henry Hare to John Taylor...$30...24 acres binding
on Mill Pond and lands of Dempsey Knight; tract allotted to Hare's
mother in division of land of William Arnold, dec...
Jno. Wiggens   Henry (x)Hare
Jno.P.Benton

487 4 Jun 1832--Matilda Meltear to Walton Freeman...$300...land
that was possessioned by her father, James Meltear, dec. in his
lifetime and of which she would have been only heir, but said
lands have been sold by her grandfather, Timothy Freeman, dec. as
administrator of her father by order of court to pay debts...adjoin-
ing John Roberts. Reference deeds of Timothy Freeman to John Roberts
13 Dec 1816 for 44 acres and 8 Nov 1820 for 95 3/4 acres and to Henry
Riddick 13 Dec 1816 for 1 acre...
Miles M. Davis   Matilda(x)Meltear
Tim. Walton

488 5 Oct 1832--Abel Rogerson to William E. and Henry R. Pugh...
$150...500 acres in Bennetts Creek running through Juniper Swamp
to Chowan River to Beef Creek up prong E to Jacob Hintons....
Jeptha Fowlkes   Abel Rogerson
Mills Riddick

488 19 Nov 1832--Mary Harrell to Abram Pruden...$30...her interest
in land whereon her father, Peter Harrell, dec. lived and not included is land whereon sister, Judith Harrell, now lives...
A.W. Parker   Mary(x)Harrell
Elisha Parker

489 17 Nov 1832--George Harrell of Perquimans to Abram Pruden...
$37.50...his interest in land whereon his father, Peter Harrell,
lived; not included is land whereon sister, Judith Harrell, lives.
A.W. Parker   George Harrell
Elisha Parker

489 15 May 1832--Levi W. Parker of Pickens County, Ala. appoints
Randal Sherrod of Edgecomb as his attorney to make title to land
sold to brother, Abraham Parker and to receive from brother, Kindred Parker, administrator of mother, Clarkey Parker, all monies
coming to him as her heir...
                                            L.W.Parker
Francis W. Bostick, clerk
George H. Flourny,judge

490 1 Dec 1832--Levi Creecy to Jethro Willey...$1.00 and to make
safe to Demsey S. Goodman as security for notes to Riddick Gatling,
Jonathan Williams, Jonathan Rogers, John, Hillory and Jethro Willey
and John Folk amounting to $384.30 and one to John Folk for $20.90
land adjoining Henry G. and Hardy Williams, horse cart and wheels,
4 head of cattle, 12 head of hogs, 2 sows and 4 pigs, 1 jersey wagon,
3 beds and furniture, walnut desk, cuboard, walnut table, pine table, popular table, half dozen sitting chairs, 30 barrels of corn,
3000 wt. cotton, 1 loom, 1 dutch oven, 2 pots, 1 spider,bridle,
saddle and all personal estate...
                                            Levi Creecy
H.G. Williams   Jethro Willey
                                            Dempsey S.Goodman

491 28 Jun 1832--Asa Harrell to Nathaniel Harrell...$125...22 acres
on W side of Coles Creek beginning at white oak in John King's line
NW to John Beeman's to Harrells Meeting House to Tinson Eure's line
E to Coles Creek and then W to Spring Branch to Jethro Eure's line.
Reuben Harrell   Asa Harrell
John King

491 4 Feb 1832--Jac K. Bunch and wife, Sarah, to Willis Bunch...
$60...Sarah's one-third of land of Kedar Hurdle, dec. on N side of
plantation to run of Warrick Swamp adjoining Easons land on S...
William Hurdle   Jac K.Bunch
Lemuel Hurdle   Sarah(x)Bunch

493 24 Sep 1832--Hardy H.C. Jones to Miles Howell...$175...80 acres
beginning at pine in Speights line, a corner of said Jones and NW...
G.G. Saunders   Hardy H.C.Jones
Harrison A. Fanny

494 Nov. Ct 1832--Kicheon Norfleet to John Granbury...$353...90
acres he bought of John B. Blount, clerk and master of Chowan Court,
22 Nov 1812, and formerly belonging to Gibson heirs, beginning at
gum in John Duke's corner tree in Cypress Branch then with Dukes
and Pleasant Babb's line NW to several saplings at Babbs corner NE
along William S. Barnes line to Granburys line and SE to branch...
Charles W. Harvey   Kicheon Norfleet
David Riddick

494 30 Nov 1832--Abram Morgan to James M. Riddick...$1.00...to
make safe to Richard H. Parker and Jesse Wiggens as security for
John C. Gordon asguardian to heirs of Henry Lassiter, dec...Negroes
Anaca, Hannah, Penebel A., Jackson, Munral and Jefferson...
                                            Abraham Morgan
                                            James M. Riddick
John F. Parker   Richard H. Parker

495 8 May 1833--John Hofler to Reuben Lassiter...$1.00...to make

safe to James T. Freeman and Garrett Hofler for notes...128 acres
where said John lives, bounded on N by John Small, W by William
Ellis heirs, S by Mills Pond, belonging to Andrew R. Harrell and
on E by land of William Cowper; yoke of oxen, 5 head of cattle,
20 hogs, Negro man Lewis and Negro woman, Pleasant, double gigg
and sorrell colt...

John Hinton
John W. Hinton

Jas.T.Freeman
G. Hofler

John Hofler
Reuben Lassiter

496 25 May 1833--Isaac F. Stafford to William E. Pugh...$1.00 to
secure to John Bond note of $400...all stock of materias...

Isaac F.Stafford
Jno.Bond

James Bond

Wm.E.Pugh

497 15 Jun 1833--William Morse to Henry Gilliam and Benbury Walton,
Walton & Bond, and David Parker for debts...building on wharf of
Walton & Bond...

John R. Gilliam

William Morse

498 15 June 1833--William Morse to Lawrence S. Daughtry...any interest left in above building after debts paid...

John R. Gilliam

William Morse

499 26 Feb 1833--David Rooks to Jethro Willey...$1.00 and as sec-
urity to John Willey for $88.25...black mare, sorrell colt, 4 cows
and calves, 10 hogs, cart and wheels, carpenter tools, 2 feather
beds and furniture, loom, 2 spinning wheels and kitchen furniture.

Wiley Parker
Belver Sears

David(x)Rooks
Jethro Willey
William Sears

499 6 Feb 1833--Henry Gilliam, trustee for deed of William L. Boothe
26 Oct 1830, to Abraham W. Parker...$55...34 acres adjoining land of
John Riddick, Soloman Green and others...

Ro. Riddick
Jas.C.Williams

H. Gilliam

500 6 Feb 1833--Henry Gilliam, as trustee to William L. Boothe, to
Abraham W. Parker...Negro, Penny and her two boys, Daniel and Ben,
$385...

Ro. Riddick
Jas.C.Williams

H. Gilliam

500 22 May 1827--Joseph Gordon, trustee, to James Brinkley...$390
50 acres belonging to Abraham Twine, and formerly belonging to Wynns
Baker, adjoining land of Jasper Trotman and Noah Trotman heirs...

W. Hudgins
George Costen

Jos. Gordon

501 23 Oct 1832--John Riddick of Nansemond to John Gatling and George
Costen...$50...298 acres of undivided swamp land, his ¼ part of a
tract bought by his father, William Riddick of Nansemond of James
Morgan, executor of Simeon Brinkley and bought by Simeon and David
Brinkley as tenants in common from Jacob S. Powell, dec. 27 Jun 1807
...on E side of Great Marsh and on each side of White O. Spring
Cross Canal and bounded on S by Richard Ballard and N by David
Brinkley...

Thomas W. Hays

John Riddick

502 6 Jul 1832--H.W. Skinner to John Matthews...$50...4 acres be-
ginning at white oak post at Jesse Brown's corner W to H. Gilliams,
S to Prior Savage corner to main road and N...
Wright Hays   H.W. Skinner
John S. Roberts

502 2 Jan 1832--John Freeman to nephew, John Freeman, gift of
Negro boy, Blake...
                                                       John Freeman
Francis Duke
Wm.H. Lee

502 1 Jan 1819--Lovey Brady to William Sears...$30...her interest
in tract of land belonging to her brother, Henry Sears, dec...
William Byrd   Lovey(x)Brady
Blake Brady

503 24 Oct 1832--James Brinkley to Nathan Riddick...$350...50 acres
that he bought at a deed of trust sale of Abraham Twine, beginning
at pine stump on side of main road, corner of Bushrod Riddick's line,
W to Drew Trotmans, S to swamp to Jasper Trotmans, E to Joseph Hurdle.
Jet H. Riddick   James Brinkley
Jesse R. Kee

503 13 Oct 1833--Abraham Riddick of Nansemond to James Morgan...$500
160 acre, Brickhouse Plantation, binding on land said Morgan bought
of Soloman Riddick and land of Etheldred Matthews...
Demsey Knight   Abraham Riddick
John Wiggens

504 10 Oct 1832--Pheraba Trotman to Riddick Trotman...$90...30 acres
beginning at a sassafras on edge of ditch, SE and then NW down ditch.
Peter B. Minton   Pheraba Trotman
Ezekiel Trotman

504 16 Feb 1833--Isaac Piland to Thomas Saunders...$340...Negro,
Treasy, 34 and children, Theopolis 3 and Robert 1....
Lassiter Riddick   Isaac Piland
Wm.W.Cowper

505 2 Apr 1832--William L. Boothe to William W. Cowper...$40...28
acres beginning at sweet gum, corner of Benjamin Wynns and John
Clark's line N to small pond, a corner of Clarks and Jesse Parkers,
E to a corner of said Parker and heirs of John Sheperd, dec...
Nicholas Perry   Wm.L.Boothe

506 19 Feb 1833--Simmons Roundtree, constable, to Demsey Parker...
$10...Negro girl, Mary, sold by court order for debts of Demsey Eure.
Wm.E. Pugh   Simmonds Roundtree

506 15 Aug 1831--Seth Teabout to William L. Boothe...$42...28 acres
bounded by land of Benjamin Wynns, Jesse Parker and others...
John Willey   Seth Teabout
Miles Howell

507 29 Oct 1832--Thomas Cornelius to Nathaniel and Peter Eure...

$35...109 acres beginning at black gum on Somerton Creek in Hare's line SE to Willis Ducks...except 30 pines belonging to William Goodman Jr....

Benjamin Saunders   Thomas(x)Cornelius
James Carter

507 1 Apr 1832--Charles Walters to Simon Walters...$500...202 acres joining William Babb's, Walters, Hardy Parker, Miles Benton, Ann Jenkins and beginning at a dogwood on Blackbird Hill, E down Stoney Branch then S to Mare Branch, a line of marked trees binding on said Parker's corner E to Bentons and to red oak, corner tree of Jenkins, to Babbs and W...

Wm.D.McClenney   Charles Walters
Thom. W. Allen
O.R. Flynn

508 12 Feb 1833--Robert Rogers, executor of Jonathan Rogers, dec., to James Rogers...$50....50 acres beginning at a red oak standing in Anthony Matthews line at Coles Island, Riddick Hunter's corner on Matthews line to corner gum on N side of Indian Old Field thence NW to a maple and back to said Hunter's line. Whereas: said Jonathan Rogers died sometime in 1830, having appointed said Robert as executor of his will, directed that parcel of land, purchased in his lifetime of Patrick Hegerty, be sold to pay any debts...

Jethro Willey   Robert Rogers
William Cross

508 12 Feb 1833--Arthur Williams to Robert Rogers...$175...20 3/4 acres beginning at pine stump near road leading from Sumerton to courthouse running NE to a cypress stump at run of Ann Harvey's Mill Pond thence up road running to a corner on Henry Hayes and said Robert's line NW to road near Wolfrey's thence along road W to Wolfrey's corner, SW to gum in branch and up branch SW to the road at Kindred Parker's gate and along road...

H. Gilliam   Arthur Williams
J. Fowlkes

510 16 Feb 1833--Mills R. Fields and wife, Lavania, who was formerly Lavinia Allen, widow and relick of George Allen, dec...to Robert Rogers...$32...all rights of dower, which were allotted to her in preceeding deed...

H. Gilliam   Mills R. Fields
William Lee   Lavinia Fields

511 19 Nov 1832--James R. Riddick, sheriff, to Pleasant Taylor...$85...25 acres belonging to Capt Nathan Smith, sold by court writ at instance of Samuel Eure...N side of Great Cypress Swamp beginning at gum at John Eure's corner and down swamp...

Wm.E. Pugh   J.R. Riddick
Levi Rogers

511 10 Feb 1833--James Jones to James Williams Sr...$300...258 devised to him in will of Henry Jones, beginning in Cypress Swamp at Gilbert G. Saunders line NE to corner of William Davidson's to a gum a corner on H.H.C. Jones to an 80-acre purchase conveyed to Miles Howell to Spring Branch...

D. Parker   John(x)Jones
J.R. Riddick

512 Oct Ct. 1832--Jethro Sumner and John Gatling to William G. Daughtry $1200...300 acres, where Mills Riddick resides, on Bennetts Creek, adjoining lands of Henry Gilliam, heirs of John Beeman, dec., Micajah Reed Jr. and running to courthouse square...Jethro Sumner
Lassiter Riddick
Jno.B.Baker
Jno. Gatling

513 9 Nov 1832--James R. Riddick to John Lewis...$675...109 acres, formerly owned by Jesse Hudgins, adjoining land of William Cleaves and John Figg on S, by John Figg and said Riddick on W and by John Lewis on N...
Jo. Riddick
L. Cleaves
J.R. Riddick

513 14 Feb 1832--Charles Williams to William Cleaves...$200...45 acres beginning at black oak stump in William Kittrell, dec. line to Benjamin Hayes line and up line of marked trees..Charles Williams
Lem'l Cleaves
Sarah Cleaves

514 14 Mar 1832--Simon Walters to John H. Haslett...$127.50...42½ acres beginning at forked pine, corner of William Babbs and said Walters...SE to red oak, corner of Babbs and Isaac Jenkins NE to path to Miles Bentons to pine corner of John and Jesse Savage...
Isaac H. Jenkins
Simon Walters

515 28 Dec 1832--Mary Hudgins to Soloman Roundtree...to stay with and live as one of his family...all hogs, corn fodder, farm utensils, cart and wheels, mare, and all rights of 1/3 of land whereon she lives, belonging to said Roundtree's wife, use of Negro Gilley...
John R. Norfleet
Eli Worrell
Mary Hudgens

516 1 May 1829--John V. Sumner, sheriff, to William A. Matthews...$328...50 acres belonging to Riddick Matthews, adjoining lands of Lewis Walter, David Riddick and John Matthews...sold at instance of Etheldred Matthews...
Anthony Matthews
John Matthews
Jn.V.Sumner

516 22 Nov 1832--Nathan Harrell to Elizabeth Harrell...$37...his part of land of his father, Peter Harrell, who died without will ...at Sand Banks and bounded by land of Mills Eure and Judith Harrell.
Mills Eure
Samuel Eure
Nathan(x)Harrell

517 22 Aug 1832--Lucretia Beeman to John Beeman...$150...15 acres adjoining lands of Dempsey Sparkman and heirs of Abram Beeman, dec.
Wm. L. Boothe
Peter Piland
Lucretia(x)Beeman

517 18 Jan 1832--Milly Piland to Isaac Piland...$99.95...Negroes, Treasy and Offa...
Thos. Hoggard
Wiley Carter
Milly(x)Piland

517 24 Jan 1833--David Outlaw to Abel Rogerson...$15...5 acres known as Bakers Place, adjoining land of Thomas Costen, John Mitchell and

a part which was formerly owned by Miles Roundtree, dec...
J. Walton   David Outlaw
B. Walton

518 7 Dec 1832--Milly Williams to her beloved daughters: Mary
Williams, Nancy Parker, Priscilla Parker and Elizabeth Rogers...
gift of Negro woman, Pat, bed and furniture, $20 in hands of Mary
Williams, bofat and chest, all corn and fodder and all rest of her
estate...
Charles Vann   Milly(x)Williams
Levi C. Smith

518 5 Oct 1832--Sarah Bond to Steward Bond...$30...23 acres heired
in division of her father's estate, adjoining lands of William and
Henry Bond...
R. Blanchard   Sarah(x)Bond
B. Blanchard

519 24 Jan 1833--James C. Smith and wife, Elizabeth, of Nansemond
to James Boothe...$635...100 acres deed to land which they sold to
Thomas Riddick, who has since died; James Boothe having purchased
4/7 of tract 16 Nov 1830 with deed of sale from James R. Riddick,
sheriff...Is same land they inherited from Demsey Odom, dec. and
is in Muddy Swamp adjoining Lewis Walters, dec. heirs and Henry
Lassiter's heirs and land of John Ellen...   Jas.C.Smith
Jo. Riddick   Eliza Smith
J.R. Riddick

520 14 Nov 1832--Demsey Knight and wife, Esther, to James Boothe...
$85...45 acres adjoining land of David E. Sumners, Hughs Old Road,
John Cuff and others...
                                                  Demsey Knight
William Lee   Esther Knight
John Matthews
William Boothe

522 1 Nov 1830--Elisha Roberson to Henry B. Lassiter...$112...30
acres purchased of John Roberts, and adjoining land of said Roberts,
Lavenia Parker and main road leading to Parkers Landing...
Clement Hill   Elisha(x)Roberson
Henry Jocelin

523 5 Nov 1832--Henry B. Lassiter to Reuben Lassiter...$155.44...
two tracts of land in Indian Neck: first of 30 acres bought of
Elisha Roberson and second of 15 acres, where he now lives, and
bounded by Clement Hill...
J. Walton   Henry B. Lassiter
Easton Blanchard

524 2 Oct 1832--Henry B. Lassiter to Clement Hill...$50...15 acres
in Indian Neck, whereon he lives, beginning at corner of Mrs. Parker's land and S along road...
James Outlaw   Henry B. Lassiter
Henry Jocelin

524 20 Feb 1833--Nathan Riddick to James R. Riddick...$80...47
acres, part of Hudgins Tract, beginning near road at William Cleaves

corner (formerly John Lewis) to small hickory in Honey Pot Swamp.
Thom.L. Gary   Nathan Riddick
A.W. Parker

525 26 Jan 1833--Reuben Hinton to George Freeman...$16...
beginning at a popular on E side of land between Hintons and
Freemans S to road leading to Gatesville and up road N...
H. Gilliam   Reuben Hinton

526 15 Dec 1832--Samuel Brown to John Roberts...$65...40 acres on
side of Bennetts Creek and bounded by land of said Roberts and John
Morris and is all that tract that belonged to Sarah Reed and on
which she now lives, which she conveyed to said Brown 1? Feb 1827.
Jas. T. Freeman   Samuel(B)Brown
Benjamin Brown

527 1 Aug 1832--Walton Freeman to John Roberts...$662.15½...two
tracts of land that James Meltier died possessed of and which were
sold after his death by his administrator, Timothy Freeman, to pay
debts of the deceased...1st tract of 44 acres on Bennetts Creek begins at pocosin in Edward Brisco's line NE to Meltears corner to
William Hinton Sr. SW. 2nd tract of 95 acres begins by side of Mill
Pond NW to said Roberts line to Hintons line...   Walton Freeman
Jo. Riddick
J. Walton

528 19 Aug 1833--William W. Stedman, Henry Gilliam, Robert Riddick
and Richard H. Ballard are bound to David L. Swan, governor, for
$10,000...whereas said Stedman hath been duly elected clerk of
court of pleas and quarter session for Gates... James Morgan, wit.

528 23 Aug 1833--Elisha H. Bond to Mills Roberts...$1.00 and to
secure to Henry Gilliam and Henry Bond $200 note to Jethro Willey
2 tracts of land...first of 142 acres joins Richard Odom and James
Williams and the 2nd tract of 255 acres joins said Williams, Eff
Lewis and William Goodman...   Elisha H. Bond
                                                     Henry Gilliam
James Bond   Henry Bond
Richard(x)Curl   Mills Roberts

529 10 Aug 1833--Clement Hill to Henry Gilliam...$1.00 to insure
to Benbury Walton debt of $900...200 acres adjoining John Roberts,
William Hinton and others, where said Hill now lives, and all stock
and household and kitchen furniture...
                                                     Clement Hill
Jno. Bond   Benbury Walton
Jas. Bond   H. Gilliam

530 14 Aug 1833--George Freeman to William E. Pugh...$1.00 and to
secure $227 bond to Benbury Walton and John Bond...65 acres adjoin-
ing land of Reuben Hinton and Frederick Pearce and 40,000 shingles,..
horse and gigg...   George Freeman
James Bond   Walton and Bond
Rufus K. Speed   Wm. E. Pugh

531 24 Jun 1833--Sarah Blanchard to John Walton...$1.00 and to make

safe a note to Benbury Walton for $15.12 and another for $60 to
said John...undivided interest in Negro Esther and her three children Daniel, Harriett and Dave and household and kitchen furniture.
Benbury Walton   Sarah(SB)Blanchard

532 6 Mar 1831--Beverley Daniel, US Marshal for district of North
Carolina, to Benjamin Sumner...$150...land whereon Mills Riddick
resides adjoining public square and lands of Henry Gilliam and
John Beeman. Sold by a court writ from district of Albermarle a-
gainst Mills Riddick, James R. Riddick and John Gatling.for debts.
H.M. Miller   Bev. Daniel

533 2 Mar 1833--Isaac F. Stafford to Henry Gilliam, John Bond, Jeptha
Fowlkes and Laurence S. Daugherty...$.50...all stock of material for
carrying on carriage and gigg making business, tools and household
and kitchen furniture...as security for bond to Willie McPherson,
guardian to Mary V. Proctor for $600...
John R. Gilliam   Isaac F. Stafford

534 16 May 1833--Jacob Powell to Henry Costen...$1.00 and as security
for notes to James Costen Sr., Joseph Gordon and David Benton and another to John C. Gordon, guardian to heirs of Henry Lassiter...tract
whereon he lives, 200 acres, adjoining lands of Robert Riddick, Holloday Walton, John Granbury's heirs and Benjamin Briggs and another
tract of 123 acres, which he bought of Charles and Josiah Briggs,
formerly belonging to Soloman Briggs, dec. and adjoining lands of
Soloman Small, Robert Riddick and others...Negroes Ben and Becca...
Wm.W. Hall   Jacob Powell
                                                  Henry Costen
20 Jun 1833--Esther Mitchell to William E. Pugh...
$1.00...for consideration of relationship which exists between said
Esther and her son, John Mitchell and William S. Riddick...500 acres
where she lives adjoining David Kelly, Isaac Harrell, Thomas Costen
and Seth Spivey, Negro Tom(called Tom Mitchell), Prudence and boys,
George and Oliver, 1 bed and furniture, kitchen furniture, all clothes
and 2 spinning wheels...
I.S. Harrell   Esther Mitchell
Thomas R. Costen   William E. Pugh

536 23 May 1833--Whitmill Goodman to William H. Goodman...$1.00
and to secure note for $6.00 to Jethro Willey...16 hogs,household
and kitchen furniture...
                                                  Whitty Goodman
                                                  Wm.H.Goodman
Jethro D. Goodman   Jethro Willey

537 23 May 1833--Nathaniel Watkins to James Morgan...$1.00 to make
safe to Riddick Jones as security as a fee for filing bill of equity
against Jordon Winslow of Perquimans and for attending said suit as
agent...Negro woman, Selah, and child, Hetty...
Demsey Vann   Nath'l (x)Watkins

537 2 Mar 1833--James R. Riddick, sheriff, to Levi Beeman...$308...
Negro girl Mary...for writs against Dempsey Eure by John Beeman, dec.
and Jeptha Fowlkes...
H. Gilliam   J.R. Riddick

538 2 Mar 1833--James R. Riddick, sheriff, to Dempsey Sparkman...

$390.50...Negro Jim sold by court writ at instance of John Beeman, dec. and Jeptha Fowlkes...
H. Gilliam
James R. Riddick

538 2 Mar 1833--Francis Smith and Jane Parker to Jethro Barnes...
$725...Negro Abram and Negro Chelsea...
Demsey Goodman
James Rogers
Francis(x)Smith
Jane(x)Parker

539 4 Mar 1833--Jethro Barnes and his mother, Prudence Williams, (formerly widow of Richard Barnes), dec. to Francis Smith...$800... 3 lots named in the division of said Richard's estate: No. 5--41½ acres drawn by William Barnes, No. 6 drawn by Pipkin of 73 acres; both beginning at sycamore on road leading from Somerton to Gates courthouse in Mills Rogers line NW to James Barnes line to run of Beech Swamp to black gum, corner of John W. Odom S to Lawrence Branch to black gum in Long Branch...and Lot No. 8, drawn by Jethro Barnes, 84 acres beginning at black gum in Long Branch to Edward Howell's line and SW to Cabin Branch...
Dempsey Goodman
Edwin Cross
Jethro Barnes
Prudence Williams

540 18 Jan 1831--J. Willey, constable, to James R. Riddick...$251.75 Negro Hasty and her children sold by writ against Charles, Ira and Lewis Carter...
J. Willey
Robert Rogers

540 29 Jan 1831--J.R. Riddick to William Gatling...$260...Negro Hasty and her children...
John Walton
J.R. Riddick

540 20 Sep 1832--John Jones to H.H.C.Jones...$175...80 acres beginning at a pine in Speights line NW to said H.H.C.'s line SW...
James(x)Sumner
Eli Boyet
John(x)Jones

541 30 Sep 1833--Henry Gilliam, Dempsey S. Goodman and David Parker are bound to his exellency David L. Swann, esq. gov. for 5000 pds for purpose of Henry Gilliam being clerk of superior court of law...
H. Gilliam
Dempsey S. Goodman
John Walton, P.R.
D. Parker

542 30 Sep 1833--Tilman D. Vann and wife, Sarah...$175...151 acres to John Willey...beginning at path leading from James Jones to William Sears Mill near R. Rogers fence in a small branch NW to stooping green pine W to sweet gum, Isaac Pipkin's corner along his line to small maple, corner of Pipkins and Susan Copeland SE to said Sears...
Tilman D. Vann
James S. Jones
Sally E. Vann

543 26 Mar 1833--Thomas Smith to David Umphlet...$55...30 acres binding on Mire Branch beginning at corner tree in said Umphlet's line W to Elizabeth Briscoe's along her line to Mill Branch...
Levi Eure
James Carter
Thomas Smith

543 3 Oct 1833--Thomas Saunders, trustee of James B. Baker and John Roberts...$1.00 paid by said Baker within deed registered, description appears more fully in Bk. 13 p. 83-84...
                                                    Thomas Saunders
Mills Roberts
D. Parker

544 1 Oct 1833--John B. Baker to James R. Riddick, as trustee...
$1.00 and to secure to John C. Gordon $1500 note...Negroes Sam, Dinah, Henry, Abraham, Edward, Stephen and Luten...
                                          J.B. Baker
                                          Jno.C.Gordon
Jo. Riddick   J.R. Riddick

545 15 Oct 1833--George Freeman to Henry Gilliam...$.50...to secure notes to John Walton and Jeptha Fowlkes...4 bedrooms and furniture, walnut table, 6 yellow windsor chairs, 1 yoke oxen, 4 cows, 10 sheep, 21 hogs, 2 casts, apple mill, trough and press, corn and fodder crop, 4 barrels brandy, household and kitchen furniture...
                                          George Freeman
J. Walton   H. Gilliam

545 20 May 1833--Jesse Arline to James Arline...$15...5 acres beginning at sweet gum at new road in a branch N and then W...
W.K. Moore   Jesse Arline
William Cross

546 23 Feb 1832--Kicheon Norfleet and Pryor Savage to Joseph Riddick of Thomas...$600...254 acres adjoining John and James Figg, Mills R. Field, John R. Norfleet and others...land which Thomas Riddick, dec. purchased of Jethro, David E., Thomas and Edward Sumners and Lewis M. Jeggetts; whereon said Joseph resides and which was sold by James R. Riddick, sheriff, at public sale 2 Nov 1830 and bought by said Norfleet and Savage...
                                          Kicheon Norfleet
H. Gilliam   Pryor Savage

547 23 Feb 1832--Kicheon Norfleet to Joseph Riddick of Thomas...
$572...350 acre plantation, whereon said Thomas, dec. resided at the time of his death adjoining said Norfleet, Benjamin Hayes and John Gatling, and which he gave to his son, John Riddick, by deed 22 Nov 1828, and was sold by James R. Riddick, sheriff, to said Norfleet...
H. Gilliam   Kicheon Norfleet

547 12 Mar 1825--John Gatling to William Gatling...$286...85 3/4 acres beginning on Riddick Gatlings corner in Eff Lewis line to post oak, corner of Lewis and Susan Boush...
R. Gatling   Jno. Gatling

548 30 May 1832--Thomas B. Hunter to Richard H. Parker...$125...
25 acres beginning at red oak on corner in Rawls line SW to Rice's line N to Parkers lot, where he lives on main road...
                                          Thos.B. Hunter
Wm.S. Cowper

548 13 Mar 1833--Nathan Harrell to secure to Eliza Harrell for $83.32 note to Henry Gilliam...Negro boy Garrison, 2 bulls, 1 bed and furniture, chest,dutch oven and sieve...
                                          Nathan(x)Harrell
H. Gilliam
James Williams

549 18 Feb 1833--Isaac S. Harrell to Holliday Walton...$350...150
acres, woodland tract formerly belonging to Kedar and Benjamin
Ballard and sold by deed of trust to Tilly W. Carr, adjoining land
of heirs of Joseph Harrell, Samuel Harrell, Creecy heirs and others.
Sam'l Harrell   I.S. Harrell
Miles Briggs

549 4 Mar 1833--Mary Harrell to Thomas Smith...$112...60 acres on
Cypress Swamp beginning at white oak, a corner in David Lewis line
running to Mirey Branch and down run to David Umphlet's line...
A.W. Parker   Mary(x)Harrell
Elisha Parker

550 20 May 1833--James Saunders and wife, Susanna, to Barnet March
$12...3 acres beginning at large lightwood stump at line between
North Carolina and Virginia running S along road leading to Gates
courthouse in line of land belonging to Lewis Eure, dec. then E...
is part of tract whereon they reside...
Thos. L. Gary   James Saunders

551 6 May 1833--James T. Freeman to John Hofler...$1.00 for land
whereon John resides, which was conveyed to said Freeman by deed
of trust, to secure debt to William Cowper for which John Hinton
and Garrett Hofler were securities...
Reuben Lassiter   Jas.T.Freeman
G. Hofler

551 8 May--John Hofler to James Eure...$1.00...20 acres, whereon
said Eure lives, to secure payment of debt due to James Powell and
for which Daniel Eure and Isaac Hofler were said security...
Reuben Lassiter   John Hofler
G. Hofler

552 20 May 1833--Job R. Hall to Lassiter Riddick...$1200...160
acres, adjoining lands of John B. Baker, heirs of Abner Roundtree,
heirs of Michael Laurence, and known as Hog Pen Lane, beginning
at a gum on N side of Honey Pot road in Bakers line NE to ditch
and NW to Roundtrees then E on Laurence line to William W. Riddicks
SE to Benjamin Hays and W to Savage's line...
Wills Cowper Jr.   Job R. Hall
J. Walton

553 20 Apr 1833--William Babb to Simon Walters...$92...11½ acres
beginning at branch in George W. Smith's corner SE to Walters line
and then NE...
Isaac Williams   William Babb
E. Smith

553 17 Mar 1833--Simon Walters to William Babb...$24...2 3/4 acres
beginning at a maple in Walters and Babbs lines SW to new road and NE.
Isaac Walters   Simon Walters
E. Smith

554 1 May 1833--Jethro Barnes of Hertford to William Lee...$45...
18 3/4 acres beginning at spruce pine corner of said Lee's along
his line to Edward Howell's corner NE to run of Beech Swamp and SW

tract is represented in sub-division of estate of Richard Barnes,
dec...
John Walton   Jethro Barnes

555 20 May 1833--Allen Smith and wife, Susan S., to Isaac Pipkin...
$220...88 acres, one share of Henry Copeland, dec. tract, which was
drawn by said Susan Copeland, beginning at Pipkin's line down swamp
to William Goodman's corner and down swamp...
H.D. Parker   Allen Smith
John W. Odom   Susan S. Smith

556 25 Mar 1833--Allen Smith and wife, Susan S. to Kindred Parker...
$85...34 acres, called Popular Neck, beginning at a gum corner of
Isaac Pipkin and E.B. Gatlings in Bear Garden Branch, running SE
along said Pipkin and Sear's to a straight course to a gum in branch,
corner of said Gatlings and David Rooks...
John D. Pipkin   Allen Smith
John M. Harvey   Susan S. Smith

556 20 May 1833--Arthur R. Smith and wife, Anna Maria, to William
K. Moore...$300...200 acres, where Thomas P. Smith died possessed of
and adjoining land of said Moore, Jonathan Williams and others...
Hardy D. Parker   Arthur R. Smith
John W. Odom   Anna M. Smith

556 27 Nov 1832--Thomas Edward Riddick of Suffolk to John R. Norfleet...$625...tract which appears more fully in division of land
of Michajah Riddick, dec. on S side of Bennetts Creek beginning in
main road up run of creek to Edward R. Hunter's line...
                                                    Thomas E. Riddick
Eustace W. Parker
J. King
R. Matthews

558 May Ct 1833--John Lewis to John R. Norfleet...$435...Negro,
Anthony, 25 years old...
                                                    John Lewis
L. Cleaves

558 21 Feb 1833--Abraham and Seth Morgan to Wills Cowper...$40...
5 acres beginning at post on main road near Cowper's Store along
ditch S to main run of Cypress Swamp to line of heirs of Jno. Granbury...
Jno.J.Granbury   Abraham Morgan
David Speight   Seth R. Morgan

559 16 Oct 1832--Whitmill Eason of Talbot County, Ga. to John Fel-
ton of Chowan...$235.50...117 3/4 acres, given him by father and
known as Quarter Field, beginning at pine on SE side of Warwick
Swamp up middle to a gum, corner tree of Shadrack Felton's to Deep
Branch to patent line and SW...
Shadrack Felton   Whitmill Eason
Ezekiel Trotman

559 20 May 1833--John Hays Sr. to son, Joseph...gift of 50 acres
beginning at birch, a corner between John Hays and James Smith to
white oak in lane to line of Demsey Jones, dec. heirs to John Walton's line to Timothy and Richard Hays to Deep Bottom...
J.R. Riddick   John(J.H.) Hays
Wm. E. Pugh

560 4 Mar 1833--James R. Riddick to James Smith...$200...70 acres
on S side of Bennetts Creek, part of tract whereon James Cross,
lived and died, and was allotted to Richard Cross by his grandfather, Bond Minchew, and conveyed by deed of sale from Richard to
Charles Williams and from him to said Riddick...beginning at main
road leading from Gatesville to Sunsbury to Hollow Bridge across
road to Holly Branch to David Parker's line along his line to Frederick Jones...
William S. Cowper   J.R. Riddick
John Hofler

561 24 Apr 1830--Abraham Harrell, trustee of William Eason, to
Thomas Eason...$41 for first tract and $20 for second tract...
26 acres, adjoining land of Charles Eason and whereon William
Eason lived and purchased from Hardy Eason; described in division
of estate of Frederick Eason...
M.B. Harrell   A. Harrell
Simmons H. Jones

562 19 Mar 1833--John R. Norfleet to William W. Powell...$400...
70 acres on N side of Kicheon Norfleet's Mill Pond beginning at
cypress in White Pot Swamp at Poley Bridge along mill path to mill
pond to Mills R. Fields line to Joseph Riddick's line...
William Hudgins   John R. Norfleet
Willis(x)A.Morgan

562 5 Oct 1832--James A. Ballard to Charles J. and Hardy Brinkley
$10...land adjoining Jonas Franklin, dec., heirs of Elisha Brink-
ley, dec. and land formerly belonging to Michael Griffen, dec.;
it being same tract purchased by said James A. from sheriff 13 Aug
1830...
Jesse Mathias   James A. Ballard
Benja. Franklin
Edwin Mathias

563 26 Mar 1833--Charles Powell to brother, John Powell...$1.00
for 15 year lease on land bounded on S by Old Ferry Road, W by
Catherine Creek,N by Nathan Cullens and E by heirs of Robert Tay-
lor...but reserves timber sales...
William Moore   Charles(x)Powell
Charlton(x)Moore

564 22 Jan 1833--William Glover to Benbury Walton...   Negro woman,
Fanny and two children, Maria and Harriett...
Allen Brown   William Glover

564 6 Jul 1833--William Davidson Sr. to Edwin Smith...$1.00 and as
security to Hardy Cross, all of Nansemond for debts...180 acres near
Somerton Creek adjoining land of Henry Jones, Miles Parker and others
being land David Boyet purchased from Isaac Pipkin and Abigail Holl-
and and which of late was conveyed to said Davidson by John V. Sumner, sheriff, at public sale...
                                                 William Davidson
Samuel Cross   E. Smith
Wm.H. Cross   Hardy Cross
Jethro Barnes

565 21 Apr 1834--Clement Hill to Willis J. Riddick...$1.00 to make

safe debt to Mills Roberts of $174.56...interest in schooner, Mary
Ann of Edenton and all tackle or apparatus belonging to same; Negro
slaves, Guy, Rachael and Mewel and children, Hardy and Askew...

J. Walton   Clement Hill
Henry B. Lassiter   Mills Roberts
                                             Willis J. Riddick

566 8 Feb 1833--John Eure Sr. to Mills Eure...$250...50 acres where-
on he lives on N side of Cypress Swamp beginning at mulberry tree on
road at graveyard at path that goes to Brittian Smith's plantation,
with his line to Little Cypress Swamp, to Nathan Smith's corner tree
and back to Great Cypress and to John Sparkman's line to road...
Nathan Smith   John(x)Eure
Jethro Harrell

567 10 Aug 1833--James R. Riddick, sheriff, to Jesse Parker...$.65
in taxes for 19 acres beginning at said Jesse's corner on Mills Swamp
and running S...
John Walton, P.R.   James R. Riddick
Wm.W. Stedman, clk.

567 4 May 1833--John Worrell to Eli Worrell...$400...4 Negroes
Jacob, Lucy, Peter and Isaac...
Simmons Roundtree   John Worrell
Elijah Harrell

568 4 May 1833--Ann Parker to Louisa Parker, daughter of Sophia
Parker, dec. gift of all land in said Ann's possession...
Jethro Willey   Ann(x)Parker
John Willey

568 25 Jan 1833--Edward R. Hunter to Marmaduke Norfleet...$800...
160 acres, all the land that he purchased of Richard H. Parker and
wife, Emeline, 14 Aug 1830, bounded on N by James Murdaugh, E and
S by John R. Norfleet and others and on W by public road...
Jos. Gordon   E.R. Hunter
Wm.W.Stedman

569 9 Feb 1833--Kedar Ellis to Benjamin Brinkley...$105...Negro boy,
Moses...
Demsey Vann   Kedar(x)Ellis
Jesse Mathias
Riddick Jones

569 15 Jan 1829--John Beeman to Elisha Harrell Jr...$9.07...1 bay
horse, 1 cart and wheels,crop of corn and potatoes, crop of flax,
feather bed, 2 chests, pot and oven, parcel of dried herring and
parcel of fowl...
Wm. L. Boothe   John Beeman

569 24 May 1833--James Duke and wife, Sophia, of Nansemond to John
Small...$75...two tracts that she heired from her father, Moses H.
Small. The first tract of 130 acres of high land and second tract
of desert land adjoining is where they formerly lived, adjoining
Thomas Small on the N and John C. Gordon on the W and William Cow-
per and others...50 acres in second tract...

John Hofler   James Duke
Jacob Brothers   Sophia Duke

570 16 Feb 1833--Mary Parker to Miles Parker...$60...41 acres be-
ginning at a pine, corner tree on Henry Willey's running S along
Keziah Cuffs to Kicheon Norfleet W along Norfleets then N to Dan-
iel Cuff's and back to Willeys and S...
Jonathan Williams   Mary Parker
James Simpson

571 30 Jun 1832--Henry W. Skinner to John S. Roberts...$200.25 ¼
acre beginning at Jesse I. Cox's corner on Honey Pot Street SW to
post on Parker's lane S to corner of John Mathews...
Wright Hays   Henry W. Skinner
John P. Savage

572 19 May 1833--Robert Parker (of Abram) to John Matthews...$18...
4 acres being part of land inherited by death of his uncle, Robert
Parker, bounded by land of said Matthews, Bryant Brothers, John
Gatling and others...   Robert(x)Parker
Mills Riddick
Rob. B. Parker

572 19 May 1833--John Matthews to Pryor Savage...$20...One acre in
Gatesville beginning at main street at corner of Savage's lot pur-
chased from Henry W. Skinner NW to Henry Gilliam's line S and E...
Simmonds Roundtree   John Matthews
Thomas Johnson

573 4 May 1833--Ann Parker to daughters, Thursey and Margaret Parker
Negro girl, Emmy; to three daughters, Sidney Parker (wife of Theoph-
heles Parker), Thursey and Margaret Parker...Negro man Dave; to dau-
ghter, Penny Carter $30 and to Louisa Parker $2...
Jethro Willey   Ann (x)Parker
John Willey

573 11 Jun 1833--James R. Riddick, sheriff, to John Benton Jr...
$23.28...75 acres belonging to Charles Jones and wife, Elizabeth
and sold by court writ at instance of John Gatling...
Wm. S. Cowper   J.R. Riddick

574 20 Nov 1833--James Lassiter to Demsey Parker...$70...86½ acres
adjoining lands of Mills R. Fields, Demsey Knight and William R.
Riddick, dec. and formerly belonging to Mills Lewis and John Vann Sr.
William Gatling purchased ½ of land and said Lassiter purchased it
at a sheriff's sale...   James Lassiter
George Costen
Thos. B. Hunter

575 7 Aug 1832--Abram Morgan to Levin Hofler...$20...13½ acres on
E side of Cathrine Creek commencing at Thomas Lank's line running
to Nathan Nixon's and others...
A. Blanchard   Abraham(x)Morgan
E. Blanchard

575 30 Sep 1831--Demsey Bond to Jethro Lassiter...$20...4 acres on
N side of Bennetts Creek beginning at Jacob Parker's line running SW
to Lassiters...to Susanna Lassiters to Juniper Swamp and E....
                                                 Dempsey(x)Bond
James T. Freeman
Henry Jocelin

575 30 Oct 1832--Peter B. Minton to Isaac S. Harrell and Thomas
R. Costen...$2250...179 acres beginning at main road W down to
Mill Race to Robert Taylor's line and SE to John Mitchells, to
William Hayes, to John Saunders line and to Mill Pond, including
mill and mill seat, purchased from Walton Freeman and the other
tract is at Old Town and called The Wharf; has ½ acres purchase of
Elisha Walton, which he purchased from W.M. Harvey, Esther and John
Mitchell and Seth W. Roundtree...
Simon Stallings   Peter B. Minton
J. Reddick

576 11 May 1833--James Howard to Harrell and Costen...$33...3 acres
purchased of David Outlaw and known by name Old Town...
                                                     James Howard
Wm.W. Stedman
Jet. H. Riddick

576 3 Jan 1833--William W. Hays to Thomas R. Costen...$500...
170 acres beginning at main road N along Harrell and Costen's line
to John Saunders SE to Whitmill Stallings E to Amos Hobbs to a Spanish oak between said Hays and Amos Hobbs and John Mitchell's NE...
I.S. Harrell   Wm.W. Hays
Thos.E. Powell

577 17 Nov 1832--Francis Rogers and wife, Elizabeth, of Nanse-
mond to Timothy Howell...$40...30 acres adjoining lands of Miles
Parker and William Davidson, known by name Dempsey Sumner's land...
I.R. Riddick   W.F. Riddick j.p.   Francis Rogers
Dempsey Goodman   William Lee, j.p.   Elizabeth Rogers

578 9 Jul 1833--Elizabeth Hays (widow of Benjamin, dec.) to James
Smith...$35...5 acres, part of tract whereon she lives beginning
at small gum in ditch in run of Holly Tree branch at N side of Par-
ker's new ground field W to post oak...
Joseph R. Hays   Elizabeth Hays
Robert P. Hays

578 11 Jul 1833--James Smith to Elizabeth Hays...$23...3 acres, part
of a tract purchased of James R. Riddick beginning at sweet gum at
ditch in run of Holly Tree Branch E and S...known to be part of
cleared land that Robert Parker cleared on E side of said branch...
Joseph R. Hayes   James Smith
Robert P. Hays

579 10 Nov 1829--Peter Eure and wife, Nancy, to James Carter...$67.50
30 acres in Cypress Swamp beginning in main run to mouth of Lickingroot Branch, up branch to Henry Carter's line to a gum, a corner tree
in Penelope Carter's line...it being a piece of land Nancy Carter(now
Nancy Eure) heired from her father, James Carter, dec...
Abrm.W. Parker   Peter Eure
Demsey Parker   Nancy(x)Eure

580 12 Sep 1833--Bembry White and wife, Penelope, of Haywood Co., Tn.
appoints Hance Hofler as his attorney to receive from John Walton,
administrator of Elisha Trotman, dec. their portion of estate due them.
Littleton Joyner, j.p.   Bem. White
Jonathan T. Jacocks, j.p.   Penelope White
Haywood Co., Tn.

581 22 Jun 1833--Richard Briggs to Henry Briggs...$154...little Negro
girl, Jinny, 7 years old...

                                                      Richard Briggs
Wm.W.Stedman

581 19 Nov 1833--James R. Riddick, sheriff, to Christian Cullens...
$291...grey horse and gigg, Negroes Rebecca, Moriah, Milley, Pat
and Jackson...sold by court writ in favor of David Parker against
Nathan Cullens...

                                                     J.R. Riddick
R. Gatling

582 29 Jun 1832--Kedar Ellis to Benjamin Brinkley...$100...Negro,
Jack, 5 months old...

                                         Kedar(x)Ellis
Wm.W. Powell
Jesse Mathias
John Brinkley

582 Nov Ct 1832--Kedar Ellis to Riddick Jones...$100...40 acres
binding on land of Jesse Mathias, Josiah Riddick, Jacob Brinkley,
Polly Matthias and others...being S end of land whereon he resides.

                                         Kedar(x)Ellis
Benjamin Franklin
Marmaduke Brothers
Demsey Vann

583 2 Oct 1833--Thomas Twine to Henry Bond...$100...70 acres former-
ly occupied by Benjamin Blanchard nearly opposite Bond's dwelling
house on main road...

                                         Thomas Twine
B. Walton
W. Walton

583 4 May 1833--John Worrell to Eli Worrell...$150...51 acres...two
tracts; one conveyed to said John from John B. Baker and Jesse Parker 31 Dec 1823 and beginning at white oak in William Brooks line
to persimmon tree to red oak in Susanna Piland's line, containing
11 acres. Second tract was conveyed by deed from Willis Piland in
1800 beginning at white oak saplin near Brooks line SE to Gen. Bakers
to orphans of Peter Pilands to livewood stake in Piland's old field,
being a corner of orphans of Thomas Pilands, containing 40 acres...

                                         John Worrell
Simmonds Roundtree
Elijah Harrell

583 13 Jan 1833--Isaac Piland to Reuben Piland...$265...35 acres
adjoining land of Thomas Hoggard beginning at a hickory running to
Sarum Creek road along said Reuben's line to Jesse and Mills Piland's lines...

                                         Isaac Piland
Thomas Hoggard

584 2 Mar 1833--James H. Piland to Jesse Piland...$235...100 acres
beginning at stake in Reuben Piland's line to Bray Eure's line to
Reuben Harrell's line to Coles Creek...

                                         James H. Piland
Thomas Hoggard
Reuben Piland

584 15 Oct 1833--George Freeman to Henry Gilliam...$.50...and to
secure notes to John Walton and Jeptha Fowlkes...4 beds and furniture,
walnut table, 6 yellow chairs, yoke oxen, 4 cows, 10 sheep, 21 hogs,
2 carts, apple mill, trough and prep, corn and fodder crop, 4 barrels
brandy, household and kitchen furniture and loom...

                                       George Freeman
J. Walton   H. Gilliam

585 23 Aug 1833--Elisha H. Bond to Mills Roberts...$1.00 and to insure for Henry Gilliam and Henry Bond, notes to Jethro Willey for $200...two tracts of land; 142 acres adjoining land of Richard Odom, James Williams and others and 255 acres adjoining said Williams, Eff Lewis and William Goodman...

James Bond
Richard(x)Curl

Elisha H. Bond
H. Gilliam
Henry Bond
Mills Roberts

586 17 Feb 1834--Abraham Morgan to John Walton...$1.00 and to insure to John Roberts debts of $4092.60...305 acres whereon he resides and on which the late Dr. Richard B. Gregory resided at the time of his death and which said Morgan purchased from his widow, Jane A. Gregory; and 190 acres that he purchased at a sher- iff's sale on which William S. Barnes resided at the time of his death; and Negroes Granville, Haywood, Sam, Robin, Jim (Jim Arnold), Washington, Austin, Hardy, Harrison, Chaney, Warren, Big Ned, Almond, Rachael, Abigail, Agga, (James Madison), Mary Sophia, Malviney, Mourn- ing, Armisted, Ailey and Lucy...

Mills Roberts
Jno.W. Parker

Abraham Morgan
John Roberts
J. Walton

588 22 Jun 1833--Simmons H. Jones to Miles Briggs...$1.00 and to make safe to Henry Briggs $17.00 note...yoke of oxen, cart and wheels.
John C. Gordon
T.W. Carr

Simmons H. Jones
Miles Briggs

588 30 Nov 1833--Asa Hill to Jeptha Fowlkes...$600...lot in village of Gatesville bought of William Eley, and all household and kitchen furniture...to pay note to said Eley...
Isaac F. Stafford

Asa Hill

589 28 Feb 1834--Lawrence S. Daughtry to David C. Cross as trustee to insure debts to William G. Daughtry and Henry Gilliam...mahogny secretary, mahogny bureau, mahogny work stand, large brass clock, mahogny sideboard, piana forte, dozen flag chairs, rocking chair, 7 pictures, brass and irons, shovel and tongs, 2 pairs brass candle- stick, 2 pair glass lamps, astral lamp, 175 pieces of glassware, cut glass bowl, 3 casters and ware, popular table, 8 mahogny tables, pop- ular sideboard, 80 windsor chairs, 30 beds of furniture, 30 bedsteads, cot and bed, large bed, curtains and furniture, 14 dressing tables and glasses, 16 washstands, 275 pieces Liverpool ware, set of china (75) pieces, 6 doz. plated tea and table spoons, 4 coffee, tea pots, 4 doz. knives and forks, 2 egg boilers, 16 andirons, 16 shovels and tongs, 2 large looking glasses, 150 pairs sheets and towels, Barouche and harness, gigg and harness, clay back colt, gigg horse, work stear, 2 milch cows, horse cart and harness, plow and harness, 15 hogs, 100 bar. corn, small wagon, log wagon, saddle and bridle...interest in estate of late Garrison M. Smith in town of Winton and in land in Murphesboro, which descended to his wife as one of heirs; indebted to Henry Gilliam for $635.61½; Wm. G. Daughtry for 9 notes of $400 as security, David Parker for $142.40, John Roberts for $120 and $500 and $120 with Titus Darden as security...

Lawrence S. Daughtry
David C. Cross

590 15 Jul 1831--John Jordon and James Costen to George Freeman...
$270...64½ acres near road leading to Gatesville beginning at dead
red oak in Reuben Hinton's line NE to Wireneck Branch NW to Docton
Hayes corner then SW to Reuben and Thomas Hinton's corner...
James Lassiter   John Jordon
Henry Hofler   James Costen

591 16 Oct 1833--Willoughby Manning to James R. Riddick...$75...
100 acres on Hilly Swamp adjoining land of John R. Norfleet, J.
Williams, Kicheon Norfleet and others...
M. Riddick   Willoughby Manning
J. Riddick

591 19 Feb 1833--James R. Riddick to Allen Smith, formerly of Nansemond, $1100...2 tracts, 347 acres, on Honey Pot Swamp, where he form-
erly lived and the other he bought of Nathan Riddick beginning at
corner in John O. Hunters line running N to Hunters and James Lassiters line E and S to Mills R. Fields and NE down new road to William Cleaves and back to Honey Pot...
Jo. Riddick   J.R. Riddick
John Saunders.

592 17 Jan 1833--Thomas B. Hunter to Thomas Twine...$2850...land
formerly belonging to John Riddick, dec. and sold by court decree
and purchased by said Hunter; being all that tract except 20 acres
sold to Richard H. Parker, and now containing 500 acres, adjoining
heirs of John Granbury, Rizop Rawls, said Parker and heirs of Benjamin Briggs...   T.B. Hunter
Priscilla(x)Twine
John Speight

www.ingramcontent.com/pod-product-compliance
Lightning Source LLC
Chambersburg PA
CBHW021833020426
42334CB00014B/608